ROCK YOUR ROLL OUT

A new method for social purpose project management

Copyright 2021 3P Delivery Authority Pty Ltd.

All rights reserved. This book or any portion thereof may not be reproduced or used in any manner whatsoever without the express written permission of the publisher except for the use of brief quotations in a book review.

First printing, 2021.

Printed on demand in Australia, United States and United Kingdom.

Edited and designed by Change Empire.

ISBN   978-0-6450217-9-0 (ebook)
        978-0-6450217-8-3 (print)

Published by Change Empire
www.changeempire.com

TABLE OF CONTENTS

ACKNOWLEDGEMENTS vii
PROLOGUE xi

Background Briefing and Lessons to Learn

Background Briefing 3

Introduction 3
Social Purpose Project Management – Context 4
The Reactive Landscape 9
The Proactive Landscape 14
Conclusion 17

Three Simple Lessons 19

Introduction 19
Consistency is the key to success 20
Implementation is about planning and doing 20
Internal skills 22

Social Purpose Project Management

Ghanvey Method LifeCycle Approach 33

Ghanvey Method Activity Domains   41

  Introduction   41
  Governance   46
  Financial Management   49
  Stakeholder Engagement and Communication   54
  Capability Management   59
  Risk Management   64
  Outcomes and Benefits Management   74

Ghanvey Method Critical Friends   83

The Ghanvey Magnificent Matrix   89

  Step One – Project name   90
  Step Two – Project success   90
  Step Three – LifeCycle phases   91
  Step Four – LifeCycle phase goal   91
  Step Five – The Ghanvey Magnificent Matrix   92
  Conclusion   97

Working the Ghanvey® Method

Ghanvey LifeCycle Phase One: Post-Budget Planning   103

  Introduction   103
  The Fundamentals   104
  Setting up Sustainable Success   117
  Conclusion   131

Ghanvey LifeCycle Phase Two: Pre-Start   133

  Introduction   133
  1001 fiddly bits   135
  Working the Activity Domains in Phase Two   137

Transition to LifeCycle Phase Three	160
Conclusion	160

Ghanvey LifeCycle Phase Three: Start — 163

Introduction	163
Day One and Beyond	165
Working the Activity Domains in Phase Three	170
Transition to LifeCycle Phase Four	187
Conclusion	188

Ghanvey LifeCycle Phase Four: Cruise — 191

Introduction	191
Working the Activity Domains in Phase Four	193
Transition to LifeCycle Phase Five	216
Conclusion	216

Ghanvey LifeCycle Phase Five: Wind-up/Reinvestment — 219

Introduction	219
Working the Activity Domains in Phase Five	222
Winding Up	243
Conclusion	249

Summary and Conclusion — 251

APPENDIX 1	253
APPENDIX 2	255
REFERENCE LIST	259
ABOUT THE AUTHOR	265

ACKNOWLEDGEMENTS

Writing this book has renewed my faith in community. I live in Melbourne, Australia, and the first and second draft were written during our COVID-19 lockdown, one of the longest lockdowns in the world. Despite being physically isolated from the wonderful people I might normally meet for coffee to discuss various bits and pieces, I was surrounded by a virtual ring of warmth, generosity, support and encouragement.

This book project started in a deliberate way in 2019, when I was fortunate to secure over 50 meetings for semi-structured discussions of social purpose project management. I can't name any of those people, but they know who they are, and I am ever so grateful for their candid engagement with my project and their authentic desire to do better for their clients.

After all those interviews, I had to figure out how to write a book, which I had never done before. I had written a Master's thesis, but not a book. I was fortunate to meet the world's best book coach, Cathryn Mora of Change Empire Books, at a conference, and I knew she was the right person to see me through – and she was.

When I finished the first draft, I felt quite self-satisfied, thinking the work was pretty much done. I was wrong. Cathryn was just giving me a break before the whole publishing process began. It turns out the publishing process is another whole project in itself! Cathryn handed me over to a publishing project manager, Kathy Shanks, who set the schedule and kept me paced. She also worked with me to design the cover and turned my Microsoft Word manuscript into the book you are reading. Thank you, Kathy, for being so organised, providing me with great advice and always responding to my questions so quickly.

Trying to express the tone of this book through images was always going to be a challenge because, let's face it, project management images are not exactly fun and engaging. The lovely colourful images in this book were designed by Len Caridi of Caridi Design, who I have worked with over a number of years and who understands me. Thank you, Len, for your endless patience and for coming up with image designs that perfectly capture and express the lighter tone in the way I've approached what is a serious discussion.

Throughout the publishing process, I had the most amazing people beta read my draft, some of whom I had never even met but who were referred to me by sector contacts. The feedback from these readers was focused and constructive. It helped me to better explain the Ghanvey method and refine the practical activities. Thank you to all the beta readers.

After the beta readers, an extraordinary developmental editor, Rachel Fernandez, read the manuscript. Rachel had never met me and (by her own admission) had no experience with anything project management related, and yet she returned insightful feedback that has helped me enormously to achieve a much better book. Thank you, Rachel.

More editing ensued after incorporating the beta feedback and developmental suggestions. This time it was copy editing. Nelika McDonald blew me away with her breathtaking eye for detail. Thank you Nelika for helping me present a beautifully consistent and grammatically correct book.

Whenever I made a range of changes to the manuscript, it ended up looking quite messy, with page returns in the wrong place and the table of contents out of alignment. I am not particularly good at putting it all back together again and I thank Jessica Curtain for doing that for me, multiple times and always with a smile on her face. You're a lifesaver, Jess.

I also need to thank my family for their support and encouragement. On the hard days when things were going wrong, they knew how to provide comfort and to challenge me in ways that helped me to stay the course. They also gave me the time and space to focus my attention on this project which enabled it to flourish.

Like so many projects, this book project did not just simply start in 2019. It evolved over many years and there were lots of other people; colleagues, clients, mentors and guides who gave me their time, their thoughts, and their faith in partnering with me to make a difference in a positive and sustainable way.

In 2017 I travelled to the UK to meet with a range of people from government, academia and the charity sector to help shape my ideas. My grateful thanks go to Chris Pond, Chair, Financial Inclusion Commission; Professor Michael Barzelay, London School of Economics (LSE); Michael Hayle, PhD student at LSE; Paul Monaghan, Local Partnerships Programme Director, Assurance; Phil Kemp, Operations Lead, Infrastructure and Projects Authority; and Andrew Seager, Head of Service Development, Citizen's Advice.

This book project has actually been two-fold: writing the book and producing a digital library of social project management resources. Therein lies another whole support crew of providers and beta testers to whom I am eternally grateful. I would especially like to thank Adam Weiss of AppDemoVideo who was so patient with my myriad of changes before we confirmed V1 was ready, Ben Erfanian of MediaStop who made sure the internet links all worked and my brother Eamon O'Callaghan, who wrote the funky theme music for both the learning modules and the masterclasses.

Two people in particular I would like to mention who have buoyed me throughout the entire journey and across both parts of this rather large project, are Zita Unger and Caryle Demarte. Both of these wonderful women have been excellent mentors for me, and I truly would not have made it through over 400 hours of development work on the book and the digital library without their generous support and encouragement. They have listened to my vision, provided feedback and have guided my course, to make sure it realises the vision of supporting social purpose professionals. Thank you, Zita and Caryle.

Many of my support community wanted to know where the name Ghanvey came from. It's a made-up name that simply comprises half my maiden name and half my married name. I wanted to do this for two reasons. Firstly, because it acknowledges the legacy of my parents, who believed in education and achieving the highest standards of excellence possible. They fostered my love of learning and are the reason I have several formal qualifications and a couple of scholarships under my belt. Yes, I admit I have a problem – I'm an education and continuous improvement addict! Secondly, I wanted to acknowledge my husband Anthony, who has been enormously supportive throughout my journey.

PROLOGUE

"Okay, we made it," said the panel chair with a sound of relief in his voice. Our dedicated yet exhausted team of four panel members had finally agreed on the recommendations for a $750 million government infrastructure investment we had just reviewed.

The panel members around the table let out a collective sigh of relief and sagged on our respective chairs, exhausted.

It was a short and sharp review for the team involved, although it didn't feel that short to us. We were locked up in a room for five long days, getting comprehensive project briefings, reading all the project documentation, interviewing stakeholders involved in the projects and then deciding whether all the elements of this project were ready to move forward.

Arriving at the end of these reviews was always draining, but a good sort of draining, because I could walk away knowing I had given my all, the project investment had been thoroughly checked and balanced and the project team had decided on a set of actions to remedy any gaps.

I had sat on several panels before, but something about this one really struck me. As I made my way home, I tried to figure out what the thing in the back of my head was. Was I simply tired after this panel because we had more questions and debates than usual? No, I enjoyed those debates because it helped us get clear. Was it the structured way of assessing these sorts of big projects that wasn't sitting well? No, I loved the way this approach supported these big-ticket items to stay on track.

Then, the penny dropped.

Why were these reviews only applied to infrastructure investment like hospitals, roads and transport and not to social purpose investment like initiatives to prevent family violence, or reforms to improve education or mental health services?

Isn't all investment, well, just that – investment?

We were supporting one type of investment and leaving another type to fend for itself. Infrastructure investment already had a highly structured approach to roll-out in which teams of people with project management expertise and qualifications worked closely with content experts on the ground. Social purpose investment had none of this.

Of course, infrastructure projects still needed a fresh set of independent eyes to review progress, because anyone in a roll-out would be too close to make objective assessments about how things were tracking. That didn't bother me. What really started to get under my skin was the fact that social purpose projects didn't have this kind of support. This was back around 2015. At this time, we had started to see bigger value social purpose packages being announced in government budgets. Social purpose programs were increasingly wrapped up into holistic, end-to-end services, rather than being funded in separate streams.

All of this made sense, because clients of these services had multiple problems and needs in their lives across a range of areas (e.g., health, education, housing and justice). In terms of dollar value, these new style social purpose investment packages were matching those of the infrastructure projects that were also allocated formal assurance review panels. I felt quite miffed that, despite the billions of dollars of investment in social purpose reforms, strategic initiatives and innovation projects, they were still treated like the poor cousin of infrastructure projects.

I began writing about it and speaking about it to anyone who would listen. I mostly got a shrug accompanied by phrases like, "That's just the way it is. Reviewing a social purpose package would be too hard to do. It's too complex. There are too many layers." I found that a frustrating response because it was underestimating the capacity of really smart staff to stretch themselves to meet the challenge.

A lot of confusion surrounds the delivery of strategic social purpose initiatives because there is no standard instruction manual. In the vast majority of cases, there is no accepted or consistent way to plan or approach these roll-outs. In recent years, some governments have begun applying structured approaches of planning and reviewing to the really big recurrent program roll-outs. This is a step in the right direction, but even this does not recognise that, for social purpose services, it's not the dollar value that represents the requisite complexity or risk, it's the community and human value. Indeed, quite small dollar value projects can have huge implications for the clients they serve – for example, a mental health reform program or a specialist substance abuse innovation project. Lives are often at risk if things don't work out.

I am excited by the ever-growing ecosystem of development for social purpose professionals. We're very lucky in Australia to have the Centre for Social Impact (CSI) that does brilliant research and offers all manner of accredited undergraduate and postgraduate courses. Their courses cover such things as leadership, entrepreneurship and social innovation, corporate responsibility and social investment and philanthropy, and are offered across multiple university partners. They are an immensely valuable part of the social purpose ecosystem and well worth checking out at: https://www.csi.edu.au/.

Despite this active social purpose ecosystem, multiple reviews have called for better project management skills to drive social policy, program and project roll-outs (Australian Public Service Commission 2015; Family Violence Reform Implementation Monitor 2018; Family Violence Reform Implementation Monitor 2019). This specific part of the ecosystem does not seem to have been addressed. I came to this conclusion after 25 years' experience in social policy, programs and projects, both inside and outside government. Over these years of observation of practices in this space, I developed well-trained eyes and ears. That's why I've put in over 400 hours writing this book and developing digital learning modules and masterclasses for the social purpose sector. I want to support the people who deliver positive social change. It's time for me to share what I've learnt and use my knowledge to support and empower those people who are working for the greater good. People who are striving to deliver on projects that will result in genuine, positive social change – this book is for you.

My discussions with people in the field, both executives and those closer to the proverbial 'ground', revealed two widely held views. Firstly, there's an assumption that existing accredited project management courses are sufficient for all project management purposes. My observations in the field tell me this is not the case and that standard methodologies largely do not resonate with the social purpose sector because these materials are geared towards infrastructure or technology projects. The second assumption is that the skills for project management already exist in this sector because the social purpose sector manages projects all the time. If I agreed with that one, I wouldn't have bothered putting in hundreds of hours to writing this book and developing the accompanying digital library of resources.

My motivation in writing this book is to create positive social change in a consistent way by empowering the people who work on the front line of that change, giving you the resources and understanding you need to be most effective. To do this, I illustrate common problems I see on the ground and provide a solution framework that can be adapted to different circumstances. I want you to learn the skills to be able to help yourselves, rather than spending a lot of money calling in consultants because things have gone wrong, again and again.

In my 25 years of experience, I have learnt that teams and individuals in the social purpose space are smart, innovative and motivated. You juggle complexity every day. But, to help you move beyond juggling and break new ground in your field, I have developed a methodology called the Ghanvey method that will teach you how to project manage your strategic initiatives with entirely new levels of competence and confidence. You'll eat complexity for breakfast. The Ghanvey method is the focus of this book.

This book is an attempt to help hard-working social purpose professionals like you to lift your skills in project management in a way that makes sense to you, regardless of whether you are in government, a charity or not-for-profit organisation, a philanthropic body, or a corporate social responsibility division of a business. The method incorporates the flexibility that is needed in social purpose delivery and the rewards brought by these improved practices should see many more smiles on otherwise stressed faces. This book is not an academic study, though, and I have no controlled evidence cases to demonstrate my findings.

From the thousands of pages of content I have read and absorbed about project management and its myriad elements, most of them were very black and white, very dense and quite challenging to get through. At times, they proved to be better insomnia manuals than learning tools. I've made a commitment to do things differently. To this end, I've designed my tools with quite a lot of colour and I've tried to be accessible in my language and tone.

In this book, I've included activities for you to try in your own teams. I use examples from the field without prejudice or judgement. The examples I have used are sometimes blended actual cases or deliberately altered cases. This has been done to protect identity. The examples I share are not there to point the finger, but rather to illustrate reality as I see it, and to try to move reality to a much better place in future.

At times I refer you to the Ghanvey digital library for further detail or an expanded form of learning, such as specific learning modules and masterclasses. Just to be clear, these are optional. Yes, you and your team can enhance performance through a subscription to the Ghanvey digital library, however if you only use this book you will still improve your capability significantly and achieve more consistently successful outcomes.

This book contains serious content about what I call 3P roll-outs, meaning the implementation of strategic **p**olicy, **p**rograms and **p**rojects that can make a real and positive impact. I know this approach works. The techniques I describe are fundamental. There are more nuanced approaches out there, but you need to be confident applying the fundamentals first. This is part of the problem I often see in the field: people trying to use advanced techniques when they don't fully understand how to apply the fundamentals.

I hope you have fun learning the Ghanvey method and this book becomes a regular source of guidance you can turn to as needed, like checking in with a friend.

Background Briefing and Lessons to Learn

CHAPTER 1
Background Briefing

Introduction

Welcome to the world of positive social change that's being driven by a technique I'm calling social purpose project management. As a concept, social purpose project management is not yet a 'thing' (otherwise known as a field). For the purposes of this book, I will introduce you to the concept as a professional and credible way of rolling out strategic social purpose initiatives across the social purpose sector. This sector is broad and exists in government, charity and not-for-profit organisations, philanthropic bodies and increasingly in corporate social responsibility divisions of businesses.

This chapter is very much what the heading says it is – a background briefing. I want to share with you my motivation for developing a method in social purpose project management and provide you with a sense of the environmental context to illustrate the urgency of more people developing these skills.

I am deliberately keeping this material as simple as possible. Even on complex roll-outs, keeping things simple is really important because everyone is time poor and needs to get across concepts quickly. Anything that's too hard to understand, whether it's documentation, structures or reports, won't be understood. Period. It's a no-brainer.

To begin, let's take a look more deeply into the context of social purpose project management.

Social Purpose Project Management – Context

As I mentioned earlier, the concept of social purpose project management as a 'thing' is an emerging one. It has no formal, accepted definition at this stage, which gives me the freedom to define it the way I see it. According to me, social purpose project management essentially means a consistent approach to the roll-out of strategic social policy, programs and projects with a clear-sighted plan for improving the chances of a successful outcome. This includes reform programs, grants programs, new initiatives and innovation projects.

Why is this important? Consider this: if you type the term, "social policy spending in Australia 2019" into your search engine, this is what comes up from the Parliament of Australia, in an article on the Parliamentary Library website:

> "Social security and welfare expenditure in 2019–20 is estimated to be $180.1 billion." (Cook et al. 2019)

That figure will most likely have increased during 2020 due to the significant spending by the government in response to the COVID-19 pandemic.

Outside the government environment, it's tricky to find out how much was donated by individuals, philanthropic bodies and businesses in a particular time frame. The most consistent and comparable data that's readily available is from 2016. Despite being a while ago now, it's worth a mention just to demonstrate how much money is floating around 'out there'. According to Philanthropy Australia, Australians gave a total of $12.5 billion to charities and not-for-profit organisations in 2015–2016 (Philanthropy Australia 2020). Grantmaking from 'structured philanthropy' provided a further $1.25 billion in the same year, and corporate Australia also gave generously, with a total of $17.5 billion comprised of a mix of community partnership ($7.7B), donations ($6.2B) and non-commercial sponsorships ($3.6B) (Philanthropy Australia 2020). That's a total of around $31.25 billion just for 2015–2016. For the sake of comparison, the Australian Government announced social security and welfare spending of $154 billion in its 2015–16 Budget (Arthur 2015), which makes a grand total of $185.25 billion floating around 'out there' at that time.

It's almost impossible to distill these figures into any definitive amounts that represent social purpose programs. Some suggestions indicate that it could be around 20 percent of these total figures (Philanthropy Australia 2020) if categories are combined: social services; emergency relief; economic, social and community development (McCleod 2020; Philanthropy Australia 2020). If we take the government spending tagged for 'social security and welfare' in total ($154B) and carve out 20 percent of the combined giving from Australian individuals, structured philanthropy and corporates ($6.25B), we could be talking about $160.25 billion for social purpose programs from that 2015–2016 pool of funds.

These are pretty big numbers and, of course, the government money will go through Commonwealth government departments to State and Territory departments, then to local governments and to social sector providers. The philanthropic dollars will likely go directly to the social sector. It seems corporate giving might get to the sector through direct donations, partnerships and non-commercial sponsorships. Across all these layers, the money will ultimately break down into a myriad of strategic initiatives, reform programs, grants programs and innovation projects that will sit alongside everyday service delivery.

Some other figures I found in preparing to write this book offer a different contextual perspective. Since the year 2000, in the social policy arena in Australia, there have been:

- 14 Royal Commissions/Commissions of Inquiry/Reviews
- 1,565 resulting recommendations
- $14.54B invested in responding to recommendations
- 5 Royal Commissions/Commissions of Inquiry currently in progress*

The vast majority of the 1,565 (and counting) recommendations end up as reform programs, significant grants programs and a selection of smaller strategic initiatives.

The resulting roll-outs will most likely prove to be stressful and confusing to the people who are charged with making them happen, whether they are large and complex, small and contained or anywhere in between. A serious question needs to be asked about why this happens.

---

*These numbers come from searching public documents, including government budgets, departmental reports and media releases. It's impossible to trace all the money through to its end allocation, so I cannot guarantee the precision of the dollar figures listed. For a list of the Royal Commissions and Commissions of Inquiry specifically included here, please see Appendix 2.

My personal theory is a tale about what we can touch and what we can't. Tangible things that need to be constructed come with instructions. For example, we buy flat pack furniture that comes with instructions on how to put it together. When building infrastructure, there are instructions in the form of architectural plans and a project management methodology. In both cases the instructions are there to make sure what you build is safe and meets the need you originally intended it to.

Social purpose 3P roll-outs have no instruction manual to act as a guide on how to approach implementation. I can already hear the instantaneous response from dissenters saying, "We don't want an instruction manual because each project is different and we can't be locked in; it's bad for our clients."

I urge you to keep an open mind and keep reading. You will learn how it can be done and how it can bring stability to your organisation, capability to your team and ultimately better service for your clients.

It may help to understand that many millions of dollars have been spent across social 'welfare' programs that are never even directed to the vulnerable clients. These dollars are directed towards Inquiry panels, courts and compensation funds for when things go wrong. According to the many reviews of some recent, really big 3P roll-outs, this is a very real problem. Think about it: when governments roll out the really big programs, often in a hurry, the best and brightest staff are assigned to the task and they are allocated a range of high level supports. If *they* can't get it right, then what does that say for the thousands of downstream programs and projects that are managed by hardworking staff without the same level of support?

From my experience, the problem is widespread across 3P roll-outs of all sizes, from the smallest, seemingly straightforward local projects, to the larger projects with several partners. I realise I might have a skewed view because clients don't tend to call me in to show me how great they are doing. I am called in because things have gone wrong, so my perspective is definitely informed by this. Nevertheless, the cause of the problems I see are common, so common that I was inspired to write this 'self-help' book and develop accompanying digital learning resources so organisations can uplift internal skills and self-manage a whole lot better.

A lot of my work is about improving the capabilities of teams to get them back on track when things have gone awry and kicking more goals as they move forward. I do this by introducing a structured and consistent approach to the way they implement 3P roll-outs. This mitigates risks and optimises their chances of successful execution. Some of the teams I have worked with have moved from being pretty much constantly surprised, stressed and reactive (very much stuck in the mud), to being cool, calm and collected because they have regained control. So many teams didn't think a life like this was possible when they were in the midst of a roll-out. Instead of working long hours and squeezing in a bit more on the weekends, they were leaving work by 6pm and enjoying their weekends. They deserved that time to themselves because they put in the work to change things around. They realised that pushing uphill in the mud wasn't sustainable and they were open-minded about trying something different.

The contextual environment of social purpose projects has changed dramatically over the last 10 years and that change is continuing, shaped by Royal Commissions and pandemics alike. This is the sector's 'new normal'. The need for greater social purpose project management skills is part of that rapid evolution and will be a critical factor in the sustainable delivery of positive social change going forward.

Let's go back a few steps to a typical scene that formed part of my motivation for writing this book. This is a scene I have witnessed too many times in many different workplaces, and is part of what I describe as a reactive organisational landscape.

The Reactive Landscape

The reactive landscape of 3P roll-outs (remember this is the term I use for implementation of social purpose **p**olicy, **p**rograms and **p**rojects) is one where staff are stressed because they are responding to emergency after emergency, almost constantly surprised things are not working out as they should be and frustrated they can't seem to get ahead of the fire. It's where respectful assertiveness turns into disrespectful aggressiveness. If this is sounding familiar, then you're likely implementing on the run and about to personally implode because you're being pulled in so many different directions at once: reporting to the executive, chasing stakeholders, running a procurement process to outsource that IT job and managing existing contractors.

And just when you thought you had time to breathe, you find you're about to face a performance audit and the only other person on the team who has experience with roll-outs has announced they are leaving. It's enough to send anyone to burnout on a fast track.

3P roll-outs across layers of government and the wider social purpose sector are increasingly responding to recommendations from Royal Commissions, major Reviews or Inquiries, very public performance audits and challenging community shocks such as bushfires and pandemics. These responses come with a political overlay and often sit alongside 'business as usual' programs that the same staff are implementing. This means that time is of the essence and there is a lot of pressure to get started.

That pressure to start regardless of the progress of planning sets up a foundation on sand. Would you build your house on sand without any other foundations, regardless of how brilliant and qualified the builder might be? The answer is an instant and definite "NO", because it would be unsafe, no one would insure you and it would likely cost you a lot of money in maintenance before it ultimately sank. No amount of good design or good intentions could stop that house collapsing.

After seeing so many 3P roll-outs in action and having read about many more in Reviews, I have compiled a list of common problems that result from being pressured to start immediately. Some of these may be familiar to you.

Thinking about a 3P roll-out you've helped implement, tick any of the items that resonate:

- ☐ no time for planning – starting without a meaningful implementation plan
- ☐ unrealistic timelines for completion – you know from the start you won't make it
- ☐ clunky governance structure – slows down decision-making
- ☐ little to no performance progress tracking – strategic alignment is difficult to maintain
- ☐ stuck about six to eight months after starting – can't put your finger on what's holding you back
- ☐ 'stuff' happens frequently – not sure where it comes from
- ☐ high stress – you can feel it in your chest and in your head
- ☐ mistakes are relatively frequent – cleaning up from them costs time and money
- ☐ choosing agile delivery – because it sounds contemporary, not because everyone is committed to this
- ☐ grumpy stakeholders – because communication is not tailored and/or effective
- ☐ poor financial management – so many problems with overspend or underspend
- ☐ low capability for social purpose project management skills – activities pile up and many get lost or forgotten

If you ticked one or two boxes you're doing pretty well; three or four and you may have a little work to do to make up ground. More than four, and you're going to need to make some big changes. Please keep reading and learning, because I'm confident I can help you.

So many times, I have seen 3P roll-outs of enormous merit fall short of their goals because they simply started without enough preparation. It might seem really cool because 'just starting' usually comes with high-octane energy, but it's completely unsophisticated in reality. The teams that 'just started' couldn't see what was coming because they had no vision. They were unable to detect when things were straying off course, as they had no clearly defined course in the first place.

Not planning also chews up an enormous amount of time. Team members do their best in a confusing environment with few colleagues or other mentors who have time for them. In a sad irony, these team members are usually very confident these same colleagues and mentors will find the time if they make mistakes. They will soon feel the heat of a microscopic lens – ouch! Not planning or underdeveloped planning can also cost a lot more money because it usually results in a timeline blow out, shocking budget problems and unplanned risks that must now be addressed. These elements often translate into paying more to keep contractors, pay court costs and even provide compensation.

It is surprising to me how many of the organisations that complain about time and money constraints are the same ones inadvertently wasting so much of both because they don't plan effectively. They go through these excruciating experiences but take no action to change, when the change needed is quite simple.

If you don't prioritise the allocation of the time or money that's required to upskill staff and introduce some elements of planning into your 3P roll-outs, then your reactive landscape will have some predictable outcomes you can rely on.

Background Briefing

The following is a short list of those predictable and reliable outcomes that I've put together from real projects:

- negative media coverage: terrible front-page stories describing how badly you did your job despite the many hours of overtime you gave and the stress you and your team experienced
- personal disappointment: being another source of empty promises in the lives of the vulnerable people you are meant to support – demoralising for you and them
- lack of autonomy: feeling that control will always be with an external agent (a recipe for very high stress)
- damaged reputation: compromising your future career due to your perceived lackluster and reactive leadership on a particular project
- setting a precedent: leaving a professional legacy of programs and projects that are chaotic, run overtime, and have budget problems

That is a list of outcomes I definitely *don't* want. Do you?

These environments are real and create a pressure cooker of stress that is almost impossible to avoid. On the upside, this can translate into a buzz of excitement with everything happening at once, feeding a sense of self-importance and righteousness in saving the world (confronting but true!). On the downside, however, these environments chew up a lot more time in duplication, confusion and potentially a lot of cleaning up after things go wrong. Sadly, they also attract cowboys, the sort of people who thrive on chaos and confusion, because there's an atmosphere of lawlessness that allows these people to get away with things that would not be tolerated in a normal environment. They can scream at staff, skip processes, huff and puff around the corridors (or over the video call) and generally intimidate staff into not speaking up. Ultimately, this means they won't deliver on their objectives and will have a very unhealthy culture by the end of things.

Hopefully I have painted a clear picture of the reactive landscape that results from no planning or underdeveloped planning in the social purpose strategic project context. Being reactive is simply not a sustainable way to operate and creates an unhealthy culture. Sadly, it is far too common an environment for 3P roll-outs.

In my business, it's enormously satisfying to turn around these sorts of reactive landscapes. On the other hand, it is also devastating to learn how many social purpose professionals live like this.

If some of these common problems resonate with you, or if you have experienced or witnessed others that I haven't covered here, then I am so pleased you picked up this book and can learn about alternative ways of operating.

The Proactive Landscape

What are some proactive ways to approach social purpose project management? You may be wondering.

Planning can seem a bit mundane when compared to that rush and urgency of launching into activity that will save the world. In fact, planning is positively boring in comparison, but here's the thing: **success is boring**. This is one of those points that I want you to take on board and embed, so I'll repeat it: **success is boring**. The experience of achieving success is satisfying but not adrenaline-filled and it's definitely no place for cowboys, because the environment is organised, people know what they're doing, and they can see ahead and be ready for what's coming. There is no big lottery-like win, just consistent smaller wins that accumulate and compound.

The teams who practice a proactive approach are still busy and working hard and there's plenty of healthy and respectful debate. However, they're not falling into risky gaps on their projects, pulling their hair out or stressed into sickness, on this side of the fence.

Effective project management even helps to mitigate, if not overcome, the biggest problem of all: having to deal with unrealistic timelines, whether you set them up yourself or they were set by forces beyond your control. "That would change everything," I hear you say, and I agree. That's why I'll talk about that later in the book.

A project management approach brings order and insight quickly and effectively. When you know what you're doing, planning can be done relatively quickly, busting the myth that "We don't have time to plan." Months can be reduced to weeks, even days in some cases, depending on the size and complexity of the roll-out.

A few years ago, I received a call, and a voice at the end of the line said, "Estelle, we're stuck. We need help NOW because we're already behind schedule and we can't figure out what's wrong." The team was rolling out a new social purpose grants program. After a briefing discussion, I realised this team was experiencing what I'd seen so many times before: a classic case of starting without a plan and falling off the rails, six to eight months later.

The problem appeared to be with stakeholders. "They're not doing what they're supposed to be doing," the team told me, with a distinct tone of frustration fusion (frustration combined with exasperation).

When we drilled down a bit further, it became clear that the real problem was that the team did not have a statement defining the grants program and its objectives. This is a simple yet common mistake. The consequence was that different stakeholders, both internally and externally, had very different interpretations of what the program was about, what it was expected to deliver and what their role was in engaging with it.

I went back to the beginning and worked with the team to retrofit planning elements that would fix the current problem and set them up for the future. The team worked fast and hard to define their program and communicate it effectively to all the stakeholders. "It's like waving a magic wand," one of them said to me. Within weeks they had a major turnaround and the stakeholders started doing what they were supposed to be doing.

The team was also feeling a lot more confident about the future of the grants program roll-out, because they better understood how to plan ahead effectively, and they had a system in front of them that was simple to understand and use.

Six months later, I checked in to see how things were going. Beaming from one ear to the other, the team manager said, "We've caught up and now we're bang on target. We're rocking this roll-out." I was so excited to learn they had stayed on track and were really enjoying their work. They also reported a much better relationship with almost all of their stakeholders.

What I did with this team and so many others was not rocket science, but it did take time to think through. Given that time scarcity is at the top of nearly every social purpose 3P roll-out, I've factored this into my approach. While my approach provides a project management framework, it's not as intense as a standard project management methodology, because I know that simply doesn't resonate with social purpose professionals.

Conclusion

Serving vulnerable people is a privilege and a lesson in humanity. It is a values-oriented calling and most people who do it are incredibly committed to it. They accept relatively lower pay, and whether they sit in government or the wider social purpose sector, they often go above and beyond to help their clients.

It is definitely time to help each other by lifting the standards in our profession to better manage 3P roll-outs and deliver consistently good outcomes. If we push for these higher standards in our profession together, we can continue to refine and create a standardised approach that is accepted and understood by funders and political policy-makers alike.

Social purpose project management skills are now, more than ever, the baseline capability measure for any team tasked with a 3P roll-out, regardless of the monetary value of the roll-out and regardless of where exactly they happen to sit in the social purpose ecosystem.

Reading this book is your first step to new opportunities and turning around your personal, team and organisational legacy. I don't want to hear anyone saying, "This doesn't apply to us." Instead, ask, "How does this apply to us?" The biggest lesson anyone can learn is about learning itself. Stay open to possibilities and if elements you're reading about don't apply directly to your project or circumstances, think about how you can adapt them to serve your clients and staff better. Together we can drive consistent and positive social change.

> **Chapter 1: Key Messages**
>
> 1. Social purpose project management skills are increasingly in demand as investment is shaped by responses to recommendations.
>
> 2. A reactive landscape is stressful, high risk and wrought with nasty surprises.
>
> 3. A proactive landscape is organised and calm. It's relatively boring.
>
> 4. Helping each other to push professional standards higher will help achieve the positive social change we all desire.

CHAPTER 2
Three Simple Lessons

Introduction

As part of the journey of rolling out social purpose strategic initiatives, there are three very simple and incredibly important lessons I will be repeating regularly throughout the book. I want you to learn them, embed them in your mind and dream about them. Firstly, consistency is the key to success; secondly, implementation is about planning *and* doing; and thirdly, internal skills for social purpose project management are vital for sustainable success.

I am dedicating a small chapter to these three simple lessons because I want you to bring your focused attention to learning them and come back and find them easily when you need a refresh.

Three Simple Lessons

1. Consistency is the key to success.
2. Implementation is about planning *and* doing.
3. Internal skills for social purpose project management are vital for sustainable success.

Consistency is the key to success

Introducing a consistent approach to social purpose 3P roll-outs, regardless of size, complexity or value will go a long way to improving the experience of teams on the ground and achieving the desired outcomes for the community. A consistent and well-defined approach can change the perception of mushy concepts to something that has the familiar shape of tangibility and yet does not suffocate the roll-out by a one-size-fits-all rigidity.

Consistency in approach can also support the development of a virtuous circle of continuous improvement if it's done with a mindset that encourages joining the dots and staying curious. The reason I say you need a curious mind is that there is always a risk that consistency can lead to an automated ritual of ticking off boxes on a templated form. This is the antithesis to what I envisage. There is nothing like consistency to build competency, which in turn builds confidence. Confident competency is what drives outcomes.

If social purpose 3P roll-outs are part of your reason for being, then making sure they are done well should be part of your organisational DNA. That means training everyone, not just the team manager. The whole team is contributing to that strategic initiative, so it makes sense to have them all understand and be capable of applying social purpose project management skills.

Implementation is about planning and doing

If you know what you're doing and are consistent in the way you do it, planning can save you a lot of time. That's because

implementation is about planning *and* doing. I want you to write that down and put it somewhere you'll see it every day. It may seem counterintuitive and may feel counter-cultural if your organisation has a practice of jumping in the deep end, but believe me when I say that effective and consistent planning can save you lots of time.

Planning *and* doing should be integrated because planning *is* doing, and you'll be rewarded with sustainable success if you do it well. Otherwise, you run the risk of playing into the hands of the old adage, "if you fail to plan, you plan to fail." Planning doesn't have to take a lot of time and it won't if you apply a consistent framework.

When I first started using structured project management elements with clients, Jane (not her real name) came to me and said, "I can't believe we didn't think about this ourselves. It's so simple." Jane's team had developed a very bad habit of just starting without planning, because time pressure was biting from the get-go. They simply didn't believe they had time to plan. Planning, I was told, was something that happened in the old days, a nostalgic period when time was available. Their own, internal project management support documents were hardly used because they were poorly understood, a bit hard to find and not particularly intuitive. The internal executive had gone to quite a lot of effort (and expense) to make these tools available, however they had missed a vital step: training staff about *why* the tools were needed and *how* to use them.

Another reason for avoiding planning that I hear is a rather beautiful excuse I have been informed about on more than one occasion and always in a rather condescending tone: "We're going agile."

Agile delivery is legitimate and absolutely reasonable in the right setting. It is mostly used in Information Technology settings because the future is literally not known. It is being invented along the way. 3P roll-outs won't work if a commitment to agility is being used to cover up a lack of understanding about planning, because it's a planning tool as well. Agile is not simply a code word for unplanned, reactive chaos. It is highly structured and has a range of appropriate controls. It's also not just a catch-up sprint of activity when you're behind on a roll-out. That's just an activity sprint, plain and simple. When I ask people to explain the rationale behind their decision to go with an agile approach and why they believe it's better than traditional planning, they very quickly pull out the 'time constraints' card and disappear!

Please do not let this be you. Learn lesson two: **implementation is about planning *and* doing**. Start to get comfortable with that notion and resist the urge to jump in the proverbial deep end of starting actions without a plan.

Internal skills

Lesson three brings us to the importance of learning social purpose project management skills in-house. It is absolutely essential to learn these skills broadly across teams and embed the practice into your organisational practices if you want sustainable success into the future.

Internal skills for social purpose project management are vital. Once again, I want you to write it down, understand it and embed it in your mind. You know the drill by now, and yes, I'm going to repeat it for emphasis: **Internal skills for social purpose project management are vital** to sustainable success for the social purpose sector. Without these skills, you'll be just getting by, feeling the strain of pushing uphill all the way, with little to show for your efforts. Without these skills, you'll be normalising the celebration of partial success as though it's the best that can be done. Partial success is a form of failure in my book and should never be normalised. I realise that using the word 'failure' is controversial and I say it without fear or favour. We need to get used to seeing it, saying it and taking the emotion out of it so we can learn from it. More on that later.

I'm not the first to highlight this need but I sincerely hope I am one of the last, because it is high time for a tailored response. In 2017, the Victorian Government's Family Violence Implementation Monitor reported that:

"The government needs to grow its capabilities in project and program management, [and] implementation planning … A challenge across the whole reform is the general lack of project management expertise in social policy, particularly at the program level." (Family Violence Reform Implementation Monitor 2017)

There are many more reviews throughout the country that are singing from the same song sheet. Many more reviews could and should be conducted on smaller 3P roll-outs across layers of government as well as different sized not-for-profits. They would undoubtedly sing a lot of the same tunes, too. A skills uplift for project team members is the simplest and best solution.

One large and multi-layered project I supported a few years ago had a big firm set up its planning documentation. The time pressures the project was subject to were among the most unrealistic I have ever seen, so calling in experts to help set up strong foundations was definitely the right decision. The big firm did a great job and it saved lots of time. It also cost a lot of money and then became out of date really fast, because no one internally had the skills to work with it effectively. By the time I got there, 12 months after the start, several elements of the project were way behind schedule for very predictable reasons, which of course had not been predicted, because no one had their eye above the busyness of their 1001 tasks. Everything was moving so fast and really smart staff were giving their all, working hours of overtime and most weekends. When we managed to largely fix the element I was working on, staff could then see that they had to start planning Part B of their project in June if they wanted it to begin in September.

Real problems continued with other elements, and the ripple effect for contractors, stakeholders, funders and clients was a disaster. I have found the sorts of problems they had at other organisations as well, so you might be familiar with at least one of them:

- some stakeholders were fed up and threatening to walk away because no one had spoken to them in a long time. The team had forgotten to tell them they were way behind schedule, and it took time and energy to persuade them to stay with the program
- short-term contractors were used increasingly as core staff left, leaving little continuity and corporate knowledge 'on the ground'
- the governance structure was clunky and slowed down decision making, with each proposal or idea travelling up through eight layers of staff and then back again before a decision could be actioned. That meant 16 layers of input by the time the decision arrived back on the officer's desk. Even saying it makes me feel like I'm pushing a heavy vehicle uphill, through mud. Ughhh!

- funders were increasingly applying pressure to get the project done because it had been publicly announced that this new service was needed, and they were funding it. They were feeling the reputational damage of being involved

There was no acknowledgement from this organisation that internal staff needed social purpose project management skills, despite the evidence in front of them. I guess that's fair enough, because it's not exactly a broadly recognised field of expertise yet. They were wedded to their way of doing things and just kept trying to fix things themselves. To their credit, they had a great Investment Logic Map and an Outcomes Logic Map, both drawn up by external consultants. The staff were smart content experts who simply didn't have the skills to bring a consistent and effective project management approach to their practice.

If I was in that leadership team, I would be scrambling to find a tool to lift capability across my staff, rather than continue to burn money on outside help and still not meet my timelines or objectives. I would want to be proactive and in control rather than reactive and out of control.

I heard just a few months ago that some of those other elements still hadn't come into service. They were more than two years behind and had no real start date in sight. I'm certain the staff would be feeling exhausted, demoralised, stressed and confused. The people who needed those services would also be stressed and confused because they are incredibly vulnerable and need the support. Those staff would never want to be another source of disappointment for the people they were trying to assist, but, without social purpose project management skills, that's pretty much the sum of what they achieved.

The moral of this story (in case you didn't get it!) is that **internal skills for social purpose project management are vital**. Without the internal skills to back up effective planning and drive implementation, you're inadvertently preventing your own success.

A line of defense for the troubled project teams above is that one of the reasons I decided to write this book and to develop a digital learning library to teach skills in social purpose project management was because I couldn't find anything else to recommend.

Chapter 2: Key Messages

1. Consistency is the key to success.
2. Implementation is about planning and doing.
3. Internal skills for social purpose project management are vital for sustainable success.

Social Purpose Project Management

Introduction

Introduction

In this part of the book, I'm going to take you on a journey that can transform your entire professional experience. This journey will help you implement your strategic programs and projects far more consistently and effectively, reduce risk for your organisation and amplify outcomes. Start thinking of Aladdin and his magic carpet.

Are you ready?

To fast track the positive social change we all desire, I have developed a method for social purpose project management that I mentioned earlier called the Ghanvey method. I developed this method by adapting elements that already exist across standard project management methodologies, auditing standards and assurance frameworks. I have tried to simplify these elements into a method that can be applied in a consistent way in any social purpose setting. I use the term '3P roll-out' a lot, which is one of my idiosyncrasies. Just as a quick reminder, this term refers to the implementation of strategic social purpose initiatives in the form of **p**olicy, **p**rograms or **p**rojects (hence 3P).

While I have developed the Ghanvey method specifically for the social purpose sector (e.g., health and community services, education, employment and justice services), the method can also be applied in broader settings because it's not reliant on social purpose content expertise. I have done this very deliberately because content expertise often hides the very skills that are essential to success. The Ghanvey method can be applied to almost any strategic program or project roll-out, so if you're working in a different field, please keep reading as you will build skills that will help you thrive.

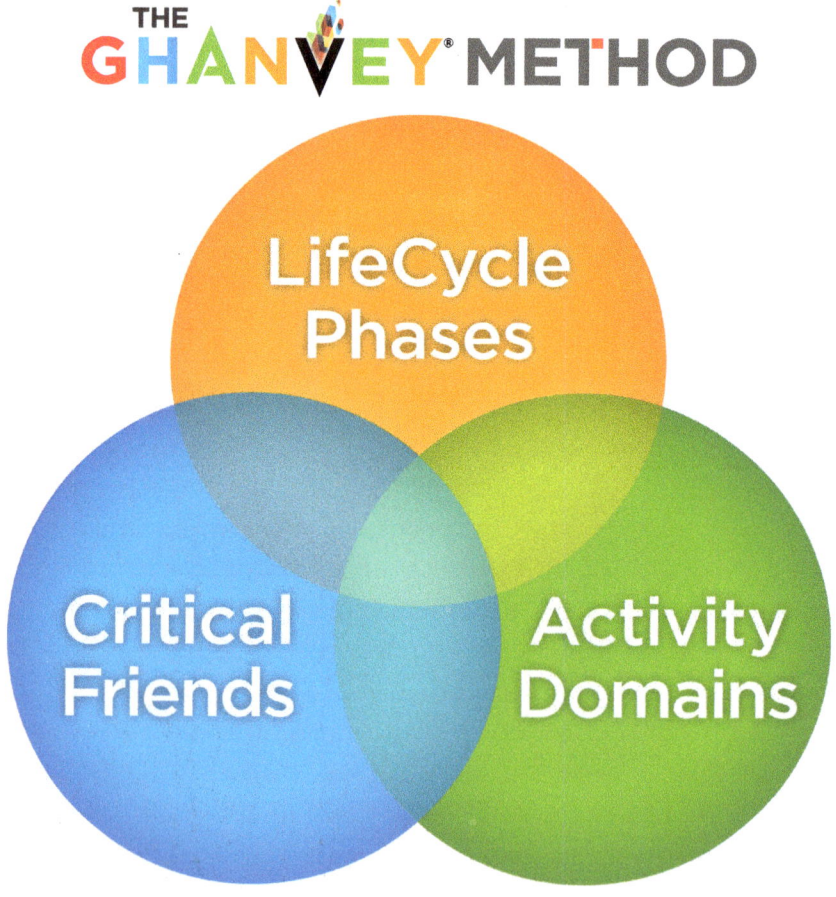

Introduction

The Ghanvey method is comprised of three simple elements: LifeCycle Phases, Activity Domains, and Critical Friends. I have drafted separate chapters for each element to give them the focused attention they need. If you get these three things right in your 3P roll-outs, you'll be on the road to success every time. The Ghanvey method is designed to complement the tools you already use, because I'm acutely aware that you don't have the space to do more work.

Along the way there are colourful graphs and tables to give you a clear picture of what the LifeCycle phases and Activity Domains look like in practice. I'll also introduce you to your Critical Friends who will support you to stay focused and reach your goals. Critical Friends are an important part of the puzzle because they lend you a fresh set of eyes and perspective to help put all that busyness into context.

Finally, you'll learn how to bring everything together in The Ghanvey Magnificent Matrix, a tool that is so versatile you can use it for planning projects, mapping decisions or reporting to project boards or steering committees.

When you get the hang of the Ghanvey method, you'll never look back. You'll be able to plan capability and resource needs and prepare your collaborators/service providers to play their part in the right way and at the right time. It will help you to make decisions quickly and effectively and provide insight about your team culture and even your organisational culture.

If you can't wait to finish the book before you skill up your teams, hop onto the Ghanvey website at:

3pda.com.au/ghanvey/

and subscribe to the library of colourful learning modules and masterclasses at any time. They are designed especially for 3P roll-outs across the social purpose sector, including governments, charities, not-for-profit organisations, philanthropic bodies and corporate social responsibility divisions. You can jump in and out, choose one or binge the lot, if you like. There's no set learning order. The tools and activities are there to help you with the roll-out you're working on right now. If you can wait, keep reading.

CHAPTER 3

Ghanvey Method LifeCycle Approach

The aim of this chapter is to introduce you to the concept of organising a strategic 3P roll-out around a LifeCycle phased approach. I'll keep it high-level here, so you're not overwhelmed too early. I'm saving the detail for Part Three of this book, which will show you how to work with all the elements of the Ghanvey method together.

Many project management methodologies will begin with a LifeCycle approach that breaks down a roll-out into a set of manageable phases, such as initiation, planning, implementation and closure. This is how it might work in practice: If you have a list of 50 key inputs or actions for your roll-out, that could be a bit overwhelming and hard to prioritise. When you spread those 50 actions across a number of LifeCycle phases however, it might be about ten actions for each phase. That is instantly more manageable, and your shoulders will come down several inches.

Phasing a roll-out gives a picture of what and who is needed in each phase. It also keeps the 3P roll-out on track because you can clearly see where you're supposed to be up to and compare it to the reality on the ground. In other words, phasing makes it a lot easier to plan ahead, see what's coming up and avoid nasty surprises. To use a cheesy leadership phrase, LifeCycle phasing gives you a 'view from the balcony,' lifting your line of sight above the fray to see what is on the horizon. It gives the fray a context.

To adopt a consistent, social purpose project management approach to 3P roll-outs, we need to understand how the LifeCycle concept works in the Ghanvey method.

In the Ghanvey method, there are five LifeCycle phases that are critical to success. These start as soon as the budget is confirmed and follow the life of the 3P roll-out through implementation to the end of the funded period, including wind-up or reinvestment. It doesn't matter if the roll-out is across 12 months or four years, the LifeCycle phases will guide you, so you know what and who is needed at which times. The LifeCycle phases are a consistent framework for approaching strategic 3P roll-outs that reduce risk and save time, money and stress.

The five LifeCycle phases I use in the Ghanvey method have names that are simple and easy to remember, as per the list below.

1. Phase One: Post-Budget Planning.
2. Phase Two: Pre-Start.
3. Phase Three: Start.
4. Phase Four: Cruise.
5. Phase Five: Wind-up/Reinvestment.

Ghanvey Method LifeCycle Phases *LifeCycle Phases*

Please don't go and throw out your program logic tools. They help you to determine relevant actions and are valuable assets in your quest for success. If program logic planning is already your standard approach to 3P roll-outs, you simply lift the inputs content and spread it across the LifeCycle phases. That list of inputs then takes on a new life. You will see exactly when you need them and how they fit into the context of everything else going on in the 3P roll-out. The outputs and outcomes will continue to be your measures of success and will be clearly marked in the Activity Domains, which we will come to in the following chapter.

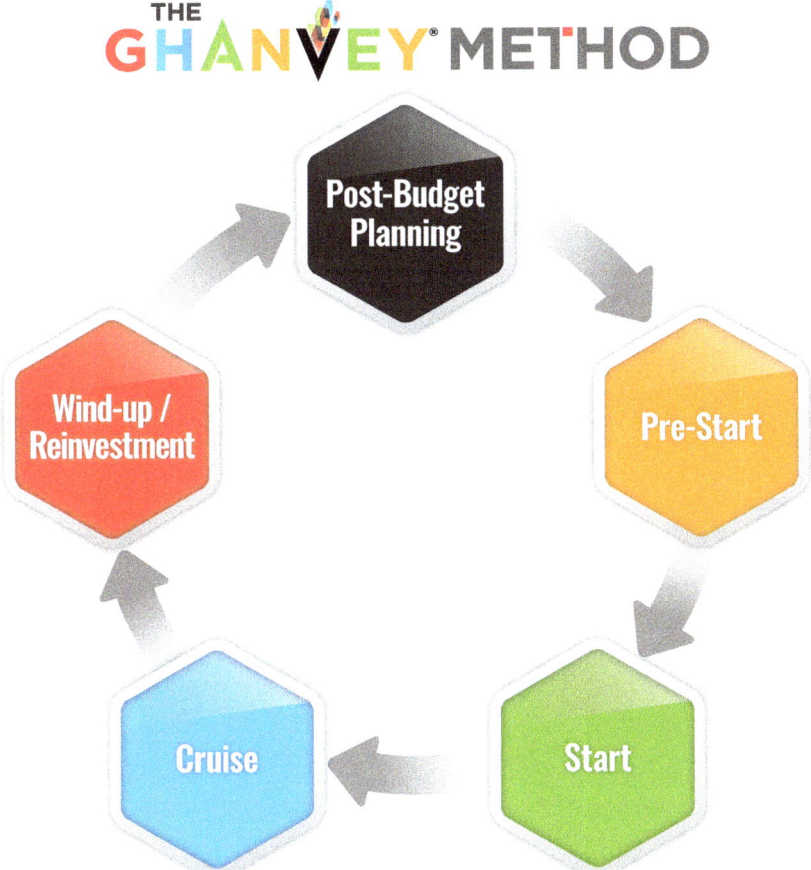

Figure 1: Ghanvey Method LifeCycle approach for Social Purpose Project Management

Phasing a 3P roll-out across LifeCycles, i.e., the duration of the funding period, is understood by funders who already work with a lot of infrastructure and ICT phased roll-outs. In my experience, funders are also usually analysts who are a lot more comfortable with tangible things. Conceptual policy and program proposals put before them often don't make sense because they are all different and can seem a bit mushy.

Let me explain.

I have spent over 15 years having lively discussions with Treasury colleagues and other funders. "They're not just units of cost," I argue. "Those 'units' are vulnerable people who need support!" My conclusion is that they sincerely try to understand social purpose funding proposals, but the lack of consistency really throws them and makes them feel uncomfortable and skeptical. Even with the best program logic showing inputs, outputs and outcomes, the how piece is still missing. It leaves them with little confidence that the roll-out can be successfully delivered. Alternatively, they fund the program and set impossible timelines because they don't understand how social purpose works.

BOX 1:

LifeCycle Phases

1. Post-Budget Planning – Plan the roll-out
- confirm the project budget
- confirm the project governance framework
- identify Critical Friends

2. Pre-start – Get ready to start
- recruitment
- systems
- relevant service providers

3. Start – Open the door on 'day one'
- check
- test
- revise

4. Cruise – Actively manage
- monitor
- support
- report

5. Wind-up / Reinvestment – Learn from the funded period
- gather data
- analyse data
- evaluate

I remember being with some clients and jumping up and down with excitement when the Victorian Government announced $572 million for responding to family violence in its 2016 State Budget. "At last!" we all said. It felt like winning a very hard-earned lottery. A few days later, it became clear that the timeline for achieving the massive agenda attached to that glorious money was two years. We looked at each other and said, almost in unison, "Changing 30 years of practice in two years? That's crazy."

There appeared to be an underlying assumption from the people who set the timelines (we'll assume that was a combination of politicians and senior government officials – the analyst ones) that the social sector could simply change their culture and practices overnight and start an entirely different way of working. Over the ensuing two years, I saw individuals, teams and organisations across government and the social purpose sector making a remarkable effort to collaborate and coordinate changed practice while also keeping clients safe.

When taking a closer look at that effort that was happening on the ground to try and make change happen, a different picture emerged, at least anecdotally. People working at the front line of that change program became physically sick and burnt out, others hardly saw their children and others again developed terrible sleeping patterns. I'm pretty sure none of these impacts were ever measured or monitored. Even though everyone seemed to know about it, no one had the time or energy to acknowledge it.

I'm not using this example to point the finger at anyone, far from it. Intentions all around were superb: the government acknowledged a serious problem and wanted to fix it as soon as possible; the roll-out teams wanted to meet their given timelines; and the sector wanted to keep their clients safe during transition to new practice.

When similar amounts of money are tagged to infrastructure builds such as a hospital, they are usually allocated four years, sometimes longer. The need for service is equally as urgent as those family violence responses, yet the people setting the timelines would never dream of setting a two-year timeline. It is simply understood there is a standard way of approaching the build, which includes a lot of post-budget planning. There's feasibility testing and strategic options testing and lots of other testing before that first sod is turned, and it is not compromised.

When the use of Ghanvey LifeCycle phasing becomes standard practice for rolling out strategic social purpose initiatives, these projects will have a much greater chance of being given realistic timeframes from funders.

My point is that unrealistic timelines are bad for everyone. Yes, we need the outcomes urgently, but clients won't be served well if the people who serve them are burnt out and the programs that serve them are sub-optimal because they were rushed. Ultimately, this kind of approach won't deliver the vision of positive social change that the projects intended.

Chapter 3: Key Messages

1. Organising a 3P roll-out around LifeCycle phasing gives you a 'view from the balcony'.
2. Standard and defined LifeCycle phasing increases the likelihood of uncompromised timelines.

CHAPTER 4
Ghanvey Method Activity Domains

Introduction

Now you understand the concept of the LifeCycle phasing approach and how it organises your 3P roll-outs into manageable chunks, we need to cover the Activity Domains that break down the project actions and bring the LifeCycle phases to life. The Activity Domains sift the project actions into themed categories that are outcomes-focused and will take you to your desired goal. LifeCycle phases are the big picture and Activity Domains are the detail. Within the Ghanvey method, they work in sync to give you a consistent (there's that word again) way of working that facilitates much better results.

- Governance
- Financial Management
- Stakeholder Engagement and Communication
- Capability Management
- Risk Management
- Outcomes and Benefits Management

Figure 1: Ghanvey Method Six Activity Domains

Each LifeCycle phase comprises actions that are grouped into six Activity Domains. These Activity Domains become the consistent basis for planning and doing across all your 3P roll-outs.

To resume the broad example from the previous chapter, we started with a project that had 50 actions. Those actions were then allocated to a particular LifeCycle phase and we had about ten actions per phase. For the current step in the Ghanvey method, we take the ten actions from each phase and sort them into the categories delineated by the Activity Domains. Now there is only one or two actions in each Activity Domain in any given LifeCycle phase.

My rationale for setting up a structure like this is that I find a lot of so-called 'teams' are comprised of only one to three people. 3P roll-outs face the same set of parameters, regardless of size or complexity. All of the Activity Domains still need to be covered, whether you're attempting a $20K or a $20M roll-out. There's an awful lot to remember for small teams, and when 3P roll-outs become bigger and more complex, my experience is that team size doesn't necessarily scale up proportionally, so there's even more than an awful lot to remember.

This structure is designed as an overall framework where you can be as flexible as you need under the key headings.

Ghanvey Method — Activity Domains — Activity Domains

The Activity Domain headings act as a reminder of all the things that need doing in any particular LifeCycle phase. Rather than running around in a panic, these Activity Domains give you a set of consistent 'home' parameters to follow. This allows you to feel confident that the key elements are covered.

Most of the Activity Domains will already be familiar to you and you might think, "I can skip this bit, because we already do that." Congratulations if you're already heading in the right direction, however, I'll still encourage you to continue reading. So many people miss the mark when it comes to truly understanding why these domains are important and how to apply them effectively.

In other words, I want you to keep an open mind. Don't say, "This doesn't apply to me," but rather ask yourself, "How does this apply to me?" That is the hallmark of a curious mind. I know I raised this earlier but it's so important I'm returning to it again, for emphasis. In my experience, having a curious mind will make you much happier at work because you'll feel mentally stimulated in a healthy way, and your productivity will improve because you'll start to join many more dots. That, in turn, will have you working faster and feeling more confident.

Learn to use the Activity Domains consistently and effectively and begin to embed them in your practice, because **consistency is the key to success**. As you become used to the Activity Domains you will gain competence and confidence and you'll wonder why you didn't do this years ago.

The six Activity Domains are connected to each other. That's why you need to organise all of them into a LifeCycle phased plan. If you pull out one piece of your 3P roll-out puzzle, there will be a disruptive ripple effect across many, if not all of the other pieces. With a LifeCycle phased plan, you can see the impact in a direct way and proactively plan your response. Here's an example that might make this easier to understand: Say you realise you're running out of money (financial management), so you choose not to hire that short-term, IT specialist contractor who was going to join reporting systems together (capability management). You're thinking you already have a manual system people are using and saving that eight months of contracting will get you a lot closer to the budget target (financial management). You'll try to get internal people with quite good skills to see if they can come up with something. Perfect!

Not so, my friend.

That choice just landed you some hefty risk. Specialist skills are just that, specialist. If you try to make do with people who are not quite up to the task, you're opening the door to sub-optimal, potentially dangerous scenarios (risk management). You've also just blown your timelines, because a non-specialist trying to do the job of a specialist is going to take much longer and significantly more so if they are doing the job on top of existing work. Add compromised project benefits to all of that because the reason the systems need to work together is so service providers can provide real-time, responsive service to vulnerable clients. That's looking very unlikely at this stage (outcomes and benefits management). Every day the new system is not in place is costing the entire service system millions of dollars in manual entries, mistakes and duplicated service for clients, potentially placing them at risk (risk management).

When the key stakeholders find out there has been a significant compromise to a new system they have given many hours of their time to support and co-design, they hit the roof and go directly to the head honcho to complain (stakeholder engagement and communication). That complaint is handed to the steering committee who are furious that this is the first they have heard about it (governance). Ouch!

Moral of the story: if you pull out one piece of the puzzle without seeing the connection across the Activity Domains, then your response is only ever going to be reactive, after the ripple effect takes shape.

In the following pages, we'll talk about concepts for the six Activity Domains that are designed to help you remember them. These discussions focus on the areas of need I commonly see when I help progress 3P roll-outs that are stuck. In other words, what we're covering across these Activity Domains is not an in-depth lesson, but an overview with a few key points.

Let me be clear before we begin the overview. I am covering the topics comprising the Activity Domains in the way they apply to 3P roll-outs, not to general organisational practice. While there are many crossovers between the two, there are distinctive learnings for the way these apply to 3P roll-outs and they need to be learnt in a dedicated way.

The box below provides a broad overview of the sorts of things included in each of the Activity Domains. This serves as a quick guide before the more detailed explanation coming up next.

Governance
- authorising structure for decision-making and guiding the 3P roll-out across the LifeCycle phases to reach the destination, eg., reporting lines, committees

Financial Management
- identifying how money will be allocated across each LifeCycle phase and how financial problems will be managed

Stakeholder Engagement and Communication
- knowing the different categories of your stakeholders really well so you can time and tailor communication across the LifeCycle phases

Capability Management
- having the right skills in place at the right time in any given LifeCycle phase, including recruitment, contracting, volunteers and training. It's also about learning from all projects, and creating a virtuous circle of team and/or organisational continuous improvement

Risk Management
- identifying how you will manage compliance, mitigate potential threats, and harness potential opportunities that could impact the 3P roll-out in any of the Lifecycle phases

Outcomes and Benefits Management
- knowing what the destination looks like, establishing KPIs and tracking performance across the LifeCycle phases to make sure the activities you're doing realise the outcomes and benefits you envisage

Governance

3P Governance comprises the systems, processes and structures that are needed to move implementation forward in a timely way that:

- is appropriately inclusive
- allows integrity to be maintained
- is consistent with organisational values
- is compliant with the law
- achieves outcomes and benefits as intended.

When governance is not properly understood or regularly reviewed (even a quick check-in is usually enough), it can inadvertently become an oppositional force that drives the 3P roll-out into the mud. Moving forward then takes an enormous amount of energy. The effort to get a decision across the line turns the focus away from the project purpose to a tug of war, pushing and heaving to make the smallest difference. Even after that hard-earned win, you realise you're still stuck in the mud. Everyone gets exhausted and loses interest because it's so much effort for so little return. It's truly awful and we've all been there!

In choosing the governance overlay for your 3P roll-out, make sure it's fit for purpose. That means having an outcomes-focused structure. "What's that?" I hear you ask. Great question. It's a structure set up with reporting lines that can deliver the sorts of decisions you're going to need; in the time you need them and with clearly defined roles allocated early. I encourage clients to 'think lean' and make sure the framework is clear and simple.

A lot of people automatically set up a range of committees for the sake of being inclusive. The committees end up duplicating or working at cross purposes, which definitely doesn't drive those projects towards a successful outcome. Servicing committees also takes a lot of time, the very thing you're unlikely to have in spades. The purpose of project governance is to facilitate decision making, not run a dance party, so be careful of supersizing. No 3P roll-out needs a spaghetti chart to illustrate the governance overlay. If you have one, take action immediately, because it nearly always leads to a slow and certain death.

Not all voices you need to hear from should feed directly into the governance structure. There are a range of mechanisms for hearing from wider stakeholders such as forums, seminars and the like. Mix it up and reward yourself with some space to maintain momentum.

I hear you saying, "But our project is complex with so many partners, we need lots of committees to keep everyone happy." No, you don't. You'll only get stuck in the mud. You need to make choices about priorities, and it may well be a trade-off between keeping everyone happy or achieving results. Last time I checked, achieving results also keeps people happy, so focus on your purpose, make some tricky choices and stride forward. You might find some stronger, tailored communication can be effective in keeping people happy.

Three elements to keep in mind when establishing a fit-for-purpose governance framework are:

1. Facilitating decision making across each LifeCycle phase.
2. Deliberately building a lean governance structure to facilitate more efficient decision making, which is balanced with mechanisms for appropriate stakeholder engagement.
3. Using Smart Documentation to further facilitate effective decision making and maintain continuity, integrity, transparency and compliance with the law.

The key message here is: design your 3P governance framework to facilitate efficient and effective decision making so you can keep the momentum going and move towards your goal.

Financial Management

Financial management for 3P roll-outs often involves a struggle with underspending because dollars are attached to so many factors, and many of these seem out of your control. By underspend, I don't mean the goal is delivered for less money than was originally planned. I mean the project couldn't spend the money *and* couldn't deliver the project goal as desired.

The money woes of 3P roll-outs are many and I trace a lot of them back to their original budget proposals, in which allocation is often ill-conceived. For example, in a four-year project worth a total of $100K, it is common for the proposal to spread allocation evenly across the four years, e.g., $25K, $25K, $25K, $25K. The problem is that a 3P roll-out doesn't work like that in reality. It has phases that will use a small amount of money and others that will use a lot. If you plan for an even stevens cash flow, you'll end up having too much at the beginning of the project, and not enough from about the middle all the way through to the end.

On any value project, you need to be realistic in your business case or funding proposal and acknowledge the LifeCycle phases and amounts of resources each phase needs. For example, that four-year project worth a total of $100K might look something like this:

- year 1 – post-budget planning phase completes; pre-start phase completes; start phase begins (low to medium expenditure)
- year 2 – start phase completes; cruise phase begins (high expenditure)
- year 3 – cruise phase continues (high expenditure)
- year 4 – cruise phase continues; re-invest phase begins (very high expenditure)

That $100K allocation might now look like: $15K, $25K, $25K, $35K.

If you start with this approach, no matter the value or duration of your project, you'll find you are more likely to deliver results on or under budget target. The impact on service providers when you don't plan the budget effectively can be dramatic.

About five years ago, I worked with a small provider who jumped at the chance to accept a 12-month, $90,000 contract with a government agency. It was a set amount, so the budget proposal was fairly broad. It was the biggest contract that small provider had ever secured. Sadly for them, they had not costed their budget effectively. Six months in, they were stressed, working long hours and unable to figure out why they never had any money. When we sat down and costed out the separate components of the project, it turned out they were putting in $800 worth of hours and cash each month that was not paid from the project. That's close to $10,000 for the year. Ouch! They learnt a very harsh lesson. While the team in the government agency meant no harm, their lack of budget planning skills saw them overseeing what ended up being an unethical project. It absolutely wasn't possible to deliver it for the price they had allocated. That's a lose-lose for everyone.

In my view, all team members should become project financially-literate for 3P roll-outs. That doesn't mean all team members have to be accountants and sign off on all financial decisions. What it does mean is that social purpose team members need to understand the relationship between their activities and the project budget, because project dollars are a huge risk point.

Having said that, you will still need a person who is clearly identified as having ultimate responsibility for the project budget (e.g., the person who signs off on most purchases) because someone needs to keep a dedicated and close eye on how that budget is tracking.

Financial management is intrinsically connected to how you implement the project and forces a healthy shift in thinking towards LifeCycle phasing. In my experience, teams that are in a mess usually demonstrate at least one of the problems outlined in Box 2 in the way they handle their project financial management.

Box 2: Indicators of project financial management problems

- allocation estimates are more like guesstimates
- allocation is not phased in line with changing project needs across the LifeCycles
- the project is not tracking to budget – it is either significantly underspent or climbing over budget unnoticed
- project financial literacy is lacking across the team
- lack of time leads to skipping authorising processes
- no one person 'owns' the project's financial accountability

A common catch-cry I hear in some parts of the sector is, "We can't spend the money because the service providers haven't met their targets." Of course, the subtitle here is, "It's not our fault." I'm afraid it is your fault. Does it make it better if I say you're not alone? I've seen lists of such projects, all vastly underspent, and yet it is not for want of client demand that this happens. It's an age-old problem that has never been effectively mitigated. Yes, I agree it's tricky, however it is possible to prevent. Read on and learn how to turn it around.

Poor financial management is actually an indicator of poor overall project management. Don't get upset, let me explain. You should never learn from a financial report that your service provider is not performing. If they are struggling (capability management), you should know because you have been actively engaging with them (stakeholder engagement and communication). This makes your response proactive, supporting them to fix their problems quickly and keep performance levels aligned with expectations. When you are using LifeCycle phases, you'll see the payment coming up and see how important that payment is. For example, you may see that an upcoming payment is important because it's pending a move to a new LifeCycle phase with additional needs and a range of stakeholders already set up to go. You'll realise that the service provider payment is not just an electronic transaction but a transformational pathway to overall project success (outcomes & benefits management). This is why everyone on the team should be project financially-literate. The relationship between everyday activities and the budget is critical to achieving a successful project outcome.

As soon as you realise that a contract payment is linked to the success of the entire project, your role is to run to the phone.

When you get on the phone, there are some things you might want to raise to get a sense of what is happening at the provider agency. I must emphasise here that this is not the sort of conversation where you're looking to catch someone out. Focus on the big picture. You're looking to get the 3P roll-out done effectively and meet your goals. Is this service provider helping you get there? Ask if they are doing okay and meeting targets. If the answer is no, ask them where they think the problem is. It might be something you can directly support or facilitate action to mitigate. Sometimes these guys need help but are too afraid to ask because of potential repercussions. Trust me, this happens. Ask authentically and listen openly. You'd be surprised how much influence you have over meeting your goals when you practice proactive financial management (and effective stakeholder engagement).

If you plan success into your project DNA, then you'll be successful – that includes financial allocation planning.

When financial allocation is working well, it can save a lot of headaches down the track. Box 3 (below) outlines my top indicators for proactive 3P financial allocation. These are part of a successful formula for achieving desired outcomes.

Box 3: Indicators of confident 3P financial management

- allocation estimates are informed by previous experience or comparison with similar projects elsewhere
- allocation is phased in line with changing project needs across the LifeCycles
- project financial literacy is present across the team
- financial authorising processes are followed
- there is a clear 'owner' of the project's financial responsibilities and accountability who is known by the team
- budget is tracking well

Before we move onto Stakeholder Engagement and Communication, let's get clear on the difference between *accountability* and *responsibility*.

Accountability is about who takes the rap for all success and failure. It's not the same person who is responsible for everyday operations. The accountability 'owner' should be internal to the organisation, named and someone who will actively commit to owning accountability.

The accountability owner is usually a senior-level person who has experience and can provide objective advice to other team members along the way. This person might chair the steering committee or be a senior level executive who is not too close to the roll-out and can maintain objectivity accordingly.

Responsibility is allocated for everyday operational matters. A manager or coordinator is usually *responsible* for the everyday operations, even if they don't carry the authority to conduct all of the decision making. It is their responsibility to navigate the appropriate authorisations. For example, a manager might have the operational responsibility of tendering for services, however, the authority for that decision may rest with a higher-level executive, depending on the financial controls in the organisation.

Stakeholder Engagement and Communication

This is the bit nearly everyone skips because they think they already know what they're doing. Most teams I've worked with have very good relationships with their stakeholders, but that doesn't necessarily mean that all is well.

Ghanvey Method **Activity Domains** *Activity Domains*

It seems that 3P roll-outs, by their very nature, have a multitude of stakeholders (e.g., ministers, councillors, government departments, local government divisions, statutory bodies, regulators, community organisations, service providers, other funders, clients and volunteers). It can feel like you're being strangled by an octopus at times. It is simply not possible (or relevant for that matter) to spend equal time and energy on every stakeholder, so you're going to need to tailor your time and approach to be effective. 3P roll-out success is all about getting support from the right people at the right time: authorisation, collaboration, utilisation.

Poor stakeholder engagement is usually easy to spot. There are common mistakes that project teams make that can bring projects undone with lightning speed. Check out the ones I see most in Box 4 below.

Box 4: Common mistakes made by project teams in Stakeholder Engagement

- project team is not clear about project boundaries and stakeholder roles in achieving the project outcome

- stakeholder support is assumed and concerns are largely avoided

- communication is one-way and the project team is all about telling, not listening

- stakeholder plans do not break down the range of views and concerns adequately for each project phase across the LifeCycle

- project teams leave stakeholders out of the loop and they consequently lose interest

Many stakeholder plans fail to filter stakeholders into relevant categories, e.g., decision-maker, influencer, supporter, opposer, interested. This is an essential step towards getting clear on who you're dealing with, in what way.

Active engagement is another term that is often misunderstood. So many people think it means, "I'll call you when I need you." How would you feel if you were played this way? That's right, not great. From where I sit, active engagement means understanding the needs and concerns of your stakeholders: tailoring communication to each category of stakeholders and preparing them to play their part. It doesn't mean inviting them to lots of meetings where nothing much happens. That's a waste of time and another mark of disrespect. They're busy too, but they're choosing to give you valuable time and input. Sitting there being talked at for a couple of hours is painful and you'll lose them fast, if that's your primary mode of engagement. Have a genuine two-way conversation. That can be confronting if you're not accustomed to actively listening to stakeholders in the first place, but you'll need to sharpen your listening skills anyway. Without them, you'll end up delivering a result no one supports.

Sometimes, or probably a lot of the time, stakeholders think you have the power and authority to do much more than you actually can. It is very helpful to be clear about the amount of power and authority you have, early on in the project. This doesn't mean you simply dismiss stakeholder concerns. It means you are clear about the extent to which you can address their concerns. A regular reminder about boundaries and the stakeholder role in achieving the overall goal is especially important as people come and go from a roll-out.

Once you know who your stakeholders are, you'll need to start thinking about when you need them. This is where LifeCycle phasing comes in very handy. You can map the categories across the phases. For example, you might need peak associations in your post- budget planning phase, but then not again until your reinvestment phase. This doesn't mean you ignore them in the middle. If you want them to maintain interest in your program or project, you'll need to plan for some sort of communication throughout. It may sound simplistic in theory, but you would be amazed how many teams forget about that peak association in the middle. There is just so much going on, it's way too hard to keep it all in your head.

Mapping stakeholder engagement across the Ghanvey LifeCycle phases brings engagement to life. You'll be able to clearly see how the roles of different categories shift between foreground and background throughout the LifeCycle journey.

If you are clear about who your stakeholders are but they're not cooperating, chances are you have fallen into one or more of the mistakes outlined in Box 4. Try a quick assessment of those points and quickly turn around any gaps. This usually does the trick. Most stakeholders need clear boundaries and they also need to know that they've been heard, and you are genuinely collaborating with them. Fake (i.e., disingenuous) engagement will be spotted as fast as lightning and will heap well-deserved grief upon you. Take mental note – always approach stakeholder engagement with authenticity.

There are more layers of sophistication you can use to refine your stakeholder engagement, like assessing the level of influence each stakeholder has. That's great if you're at that level, but make sure you're doing the fundamentals really well and consistently before heading into anything more intense.

When the teams I work with are handling their stakeholder engagement well, it looks like the picture outlined in Box 5, below.

> **Box 5: Indicators of confident 3P Stakeholder Engagement**
>
> - project team is clear about the project boundaries, what can be achieved and stakeholder roles in supporting the outcome
> - stakeholder map has been developed via adequate consultation to determine the range of views and concerns about this project
> - stakeholder plan is up to date and acknowledges different needs during different LifeCycle phases
> - communication is two-way and consistent because the team listens and incorporates feedback and stakeholders can see this is happening
> - communication is timely and tailored to each stakeholder category
> - stakeholders are kept in the loop and consequently maintain interest
> - stakeholders report respectful treatment, even if they don't agree with the project's development

Capability Management

Capability is about having the right environment and skills to manage the project effectively across the following three tiers:

- a capable organisation
- a capable team
- capable service providers

Capable organisation

The first questions I ask myself when I assess a 3P roll-out that's stuck are: is the organisation skilled at implementing projects? Does it have a good culture that fosters accountability and leadership? The answer is usually somewhere between yes and no.

An organisation or agency that is not skilled or equipped for a successful 3P roll-out can be identified pretty quickly by just sitting on a chair and watching the environment unfold. There's often a lot of rushing about and you just catch the ends of phrases as people push past you. "Don't worry about that part, just get it up the line!" or "If you don't get that done by four o'clock, we're dead." It has the feel of the Wild West and the cowboys are out in force! Cowboys love chaos and the lawlessness that comes with living on the edge. They can order people around and get what they want. Who cares about the rules? This is an emergency! Get in their way and you'll likely be squashed. Sound familiar? It shouldn't, but it probably does.

Box 6 (below) outlines the most common factors I've seen for identifying an organisation that is not skilled or equipped for successful 3P roll-outs.

> **Box 6: Organisational giveaways for poor 3P roll-out capability**
>
> - the organisation does not consistently learn from its previous projects
> - leadership is generally reactive with no time to plan and many emergencies
> - the budget is either significantly underspent or overspent
> - the Capability Needs Plan for this project either doesn't exist or is seriously underdeveloped (e.g., stating 'we need two staff' without identifying what sort of skills these staff need to have)
> - there is no plan to develop the needed skillsets in the project staff

So many 3P roll-outs only partially succeed or completely fall apart because the project team is pushing uphill in an organisation that lacks structure or consistency in the way projects are rolled out.

Adopting the Ghanvey method can calm down the chaos and bring order to the everyday. A capable organisation can demonstrate a consistent, everyday way of doing things that facilitates the job being done effectively. This has nothing to do with the size of an organisation, it's about a culture of being proactive rather than reactive. The Ghanvey method opens up forward vision so you see ahead to what skills you'll need. That means you'll have time to fill gaps and enjoy the benefits of continuity.

In Box 7 (below), I have listed the most common identifiers that I've seen in capable organisations that have consistent 3P roll-out success.

> **Box 7: Identifiers of good organisational capability for 3P roll-outs**
>
> - systems and processes are in place to facilitate the job being done effectively
> - standard good governance for project and program management exists
> - a development plan exists for team members to learn the skills they need to manage and successfully implement strategic initiatives
> - there's embedded learning from previous projects — good and bad — to support an environment of continuous improvement

Capable team

A capable team is one that is available when you need them and in possession of the skills and experience to match the needs of the project. That means a mix of content, project management and administration expertise. You'll also need to include capability for big picture and detail in your skills mix, because both are needed across all the LifeCycle phases. A good project manager will know their way around each of the six Activity Domains and be able to sync them with the LifeCycle phasing approach. Capable teams don't fall apart when a key team member leaves, because they are all project management-literate, and they already planned for that eventuality.

Leaving all the project management expertise with one person doesn't make sense. It's a huge burden for a single person to carry and a very high risk to the project if they get sick or leave. Okay, I get it, a lot of 'teams' are one person. In that case, you should be able to access mentors and/or Critical Friends for support. If your team really is a team, then of course you'll need a project manager to oversee and guide the full operation, but every person in that team should be professionally skilled at social purpose project management. An important part of the success you're looking for is about working effectively together. Information asymmetry when it comes to applying project management skills is simply not an effective way of working.

In Box 8 (below) are my top indicators of a capable 3P roll-out team.

> **Box 8: A 3P capable team can demonstrate these points**
>
> - strong experience successfully implementing a similar project or program
>
> - resources are in place when needed (e.g., if specialist staff/contractors are needed for a particular phase, early planning lines them up to be available on time)
>
> - a commitment to working with service providers early to facilitate the best roll-out
>
> - tracking of progress on financial and outcomes indicators is established
>
> - most of the team is social purpose project management literate
>
> - access to mentors, Critical Friends and relevant training is enabled

Capable service providers

If you are relying on service providers to roll out your implementation, you will need to make sure they're up to the job as well. Having known them for years is not the best measure of their suitability. People come and go from organisations, so the quality can vary. That's normal, by the way. It means you need to check in to make sure they can serve your 3P roll-out well. The elements you'll need to look out for are pretty much the same as those in your own organisation and team:

- proactive leadership
- systems to facilitate continuous improvement such as mentors, Critical Friends and measures that enable learning from all 3P roll-outs
- skilled teams with development plans

If your service provider or collaboration partner is missing any one of these elements and you're committed to working with them (i.e., you've already signed a contract), you probably need to be planning how you'll support their development. This is critical to a successful 3P roll-out.

You're all working towards the same goal, so you might need to spend more money on a handful of providers to support their delivery. I know they signed a contract and are supposed to manage their side of the bargain, but 'stuff' can happen to anyone. A lot of people stick their proverbial heels in the ground and point to the contract. I encourage active support, because, at the end of the day, it's either support the provider or don't meet the goals. If the goal is ultimately to support vulnerable clients, what's more important? Help them to help you.

Risk Management

Eyes glazing over are a common feature of any mention of risk management during a 3P roll-out discussion, no matter how badly the project is stuck. Risk is not sexy, it's not well-understood and it leads to a lot of avoidance. Sometimes I see an arm go up with a finger pointing at the end of it, directing me a long way away to the person who deals with risk. One time, working on a project that was very stuck, I found myself heading towards the toilets to talk to that person. "What a beautiful metaphor for the way this place handles risk," I thought to myself. "They just flush it down the toilet." The desk I was looking for was right next door to the toilets, confirming my view that risk had drawn the shortest straw possible in that particular hierarchy.

Poor risk management is like watching a movie with blurred vision. It's quite off-putting and can make you feel sick. All the bits and pieces are right in front of you, but it's really hard to make them out. You can't tell the difference between the villain and the good guy, because, with blurred vision, they all look the same.

How do you know if you're a sloppy risk manager? Well, for starters, if you don't think or talk about risk, that's the first indicator you're not managing it. Risk is still there whether you manage it or not, so you need to find out what's happening with it. Are you flushing it down the toilet, too?

While I believe it is a good idea to have a dedicated risk officer or manager, especially on a large project, it will only achieve part success if others in the team are not 'risk-literate' and contribute to identification and problem solving around risk. Team members are the eyes and ears of the project, they know what is working and what is not working. That's valuable knowledge and needs to be harnessed if you're going to successfully mitigate risk and achieve successful outcomes.

After almost 20 years of working directly with policies, programs and projects and almost 10 years of supporting others to lift their performance, I share the little blacklist of indicators I have for spotting an underdeveloped risk environment in a social purpose roll-out in Box 8, below.

If any of the indicators are familiar to you, or you're not sure, then you're not managing risk effectively. That's probably why so many emergencies erupt in your environment and it's probably why you nearly always get stuck somewhere in your 3P roll-out.

Box 9: indicators of an underdeveloped risk environment

- there is no overall risk framework
- the risk register (if it exists) is out of date
- risk identification and management are allocated to only one person and other team members don't contribute
- understanding of risk and how it impacts the Activity Domains at each LifeCycle phase is not well-understood across the project team
- focus is on compliance at the expense of performance
- risk discussion is not part of decision making
- there is little evidence of healthy challenges to assumptions and decisions

To their credit, most social 3P roll-outs I've worked with have compliance risk covered because they have to. It's the law. In my experience, however, performance risk is not covered nearly as well, because it's not seen as a necessity and is sometimes even viewed as a bit of a luxury. Despite experiencing a myriad of emergencies springing up all around them and the chaos that ensues, some people simply don't join the dots. "You won't believe it, we didn't get all the money," or "You won't believe it, Anna just announced she's leaving. What are we going to do now?" Believe it. Stuff happens, it's very predictable and you can plan for it. So many people think this panic is just normal, it's always like this. Let me tell you now, it might be your normal, but it is not normal. It's simply poor risk management and you can turn it around.

To begin with, think about risk as a pair of clear vision glasses. That's right: put your glasses on and begin to see what you didn't see before. These glasses are clear and show you exactly what's before you: compliance, threats and opportunities.

Box 10: Risk is primarily about three things:

- **compliance** – legislation, regulations, by-laws, contracts, service agreements, partnership agreements
- **threats (or downside risk)** – things that might go wrong and have negative consequences for your project or program
- **opportunities (or upside risk)** – stars that might align to make your 3P roll-out better

The reason why you need to manage risk is that risk is connected to everything, and I mean everything; every Activity Domain and every action in every Activity Domain. I don't mean to be overly dramatic or make you too scared to get out of bed, but you need to understand how risk connects. It's actually pretty simple. When it comes to threats, otherwise known as downside risk, ask four questions of each Activity Domain, across each of the LifeCycle phases. The four questions are in Box 11, below.

> **Simple Downside Risk Questions**
> 1. What can go wrong?
> 2. What is the likelihood that this could go wrong?
> 3. What would be the impact (i.e., ripple effect across the Activity Domains) if this did go wrong?
> 4. What would we do if this happened?

For example, I talked earlier about the problems that arise with financial management when payments can't be made because a service provider hasn't met targets. Let's have an overly simple discussion about service provider contracts during the post-budget planning LifeCycle phase, in order to flush out problems that might cause trouble as we progress the roll-out.

1. What could go wrong?
    a) *The performance agreement / contract has set unrealistic KPIs*
    b) *A key staff member at the service provider could leave and there might be a period of months before the gap is filled, then a few more months while the new person learns the job*
    c) *Changed practice reform is proving more difficult to introduce than initially predicted*
2. What is the likelihood of this going wrong? (e.g., low, medium, high)
    a) *Implementing an unrealistic performance agreement: medium to high, because the agreement*

> *is standard, and everyone already knows the timelines and service volume are unrealistic*
>
> b) *Staff member leaving: medium, because staff turnover happens and should always be expected*
>
> c) *Change practice reform proves challenging: medium to high, because everyone already knows that changing embedded practice takes time and intensive effort to turn around*

3. What would be the impact if these things went wrong?

    a) *Unrealistic performance agreement: Service provider won't meet targets; team won't spend money; money can't be held over; less clients are served; stakeholders are grumpy; outcomes and benefits are compromised; your reputation is damaged (impact is across all Activity Domains)*

    b) *Staff member leaving: as above*

    c) *Complexity of changed practice reform: delays that trigger all of the impacts in a) above*

4. What would we do if these things happened?

    a) *Support service provider to:*

      i) skill up

      ii) get mentoring from a service that is doing well

      iii) vary the service agreement.

You have to know what you can and can't do from an organisational perspective and understand which levers you can pull. Once you've answered the first question, you'll already know where your key performance risks are located, so you can keep a close eye on them. Project team members are usually well placed to answer question two if they understand how to identify risk. If you have a high rating on likelihood, it's a flag for immediate action. The answer to question four will give you a sense of how much time it's going to take you to fix the problem after it happens. This should be good motivation to keep the roll-out tracking positively, through prevention.

The answer to question three will give you a clear illustration of the ripple effect. When one thing goes wrong, lots of other things are impacted right across the Activity Domains. While the team manager will be responsible for overall operational risk, it is important for the whole team to be risk-literate. By risk-literate, I mean that team members should understand risk, know how to identify it, mitigate it and respond. A general idea of good and bad is not risk management.

A virtual risk seminar I attended recently had a guest executive from a social policy government department. The executive was describing a simple example of risk management that went something like this: the procurement team had several large tender specifications to release before Christmas. The risk executive asked them how they would manage responding to queries if they were about to lose most of the team to summer holidays. They hadn't thought of that. Great save by the risk executive, reinforcing the simple oversights that compound into serious problems.

I asked a question in the chat box about what tools that department used to educate staff about risk. The executive didn't blink when responding, "Estelle, our risk response is so well-developed, embedded and mature that we don't need anything specific. Project discussions incorporate risk all the time. We've moved on from having dedicated risk discussions. That's not done anymore." At this point, my jaw almost hit the floor. The example from their procurement team, provided only minutes before, clearly demonstrated that risk was not discussed or managed particularly effectively among rank-and-file staff. Clearly, from the example proffered, risk was still perceived as something related to significant events or issues and not relevant to everyday tasks.

If you read any reports from the Ombudsman's Office or performance audits from the Auditor's Office about major reviews of failed program delivery, you will note a very clear pattern. Inconsequential mistakes, mishaps and misses add up to often life-threatening catastrophes. Deliberate risk education is very important for rank-and-file staff so they can better self-manage their own patch.

Sort of including or generally including risk amorphously in discussion doesn't cut it, in my book (pardon the pun). Risk discussion needs to be dedicated and deliberate. By having a relatively simple discussion around the four questions I mentioned earlier, you will shift to a proactive approach and reduce the number of emergencies that arise. A risk profile can change significantly across different LifeCycle phases, so it's very important to test the questions as you transition from one phase to the next.

Less time is spent considering upside risk, because problems tend to be more immediate (and tangible) than opportunities. Upside risk can give your 3P roll-out a serious boost. It's extraordinary how teams can come up with proactive plans to enhance the resources they have and better engage with stakeholders or build capability. I encourage you to consider another broad conversation about opportunities or upside risk to enhance the likelihood of your 3P roll-out's success.

Ghanvey Method — Activity Domains — Activity Domains

> **Simple Upside Risk Questions**
> 1. What could work better?
> 2. What is the likelihood that this could happen?
> 3. What would be the impact if that happened?
> 4. How do we facilitate that happening?

Let's try these out using the same example as above. It's a service reform program with lots of service providers who have clients that are difficult to engage.

1. What could work better? (than just signing contracts with the service provider and sending them on their way)
    a) *service provider support networks to share what works well*
    b) *service provider training seminars*
    c) *service provider access to social project management resources*

2. What is the likelihood of this happening?
    a) *service provider support networks: high, as the team could organise a regular event*
    b) *service provider training seminars: medium, but would have to check the budget*
    c) *service provider access to social project management resources: medium to high, a cost-effective training solution*

3. What would be the impact if that happened?
    - service providers would meet their targets, team could spend their money, maximum numbers of clients could be served, outcomes would be met,

benefits would be achieved, and the project team would get accolades

4. How do we facilitate that happening?
   - check in with service providers and ask them to test sharing practices in network clusters once a month
   - provide training seminars upon contract signing to skill up on known problem areas
   - provide access to Ghanvey resources

Even though this is an overly simple example, it is one that is real enough and undoubtedly resonates with a number of people. What should be clear is how much difference proactive planning can make. It's so important to ask the question and have a deliberate discussion about the bigger risk context. Map out risk, both downside and upside, across the LifeCycle phases where you can see them in context and where you have a line of sight to your proverbial roll-out horizon. This makes it much easier to take proactive action.

If you're running a larger 3P roll-out with a number of partners, it automatically means more things might go wrong, so it would be wise to set up a simple risk register. A risk register should identify at least these elements:

- the problem
- a likelihood assessment
- the mitigation actions
- a person responsible for the actions
- a timeline

If you want a template for an easy risk register that includes both upside and downside risk, jump onto the **website** at **3pda.com.au/ghanvey/** and go to the Resources tab. It's free because I just want people to use and improve their practice. Go for your life!

You should become familiar with the risk environment outlined in Box 13, below:

> **Box 13: Indicators of a robust 3P risk environment**
> - there is an overall risk framework
> - there is an up-to-date risk register that balances compliance and performance risk
> - the team manager is risk confident
> - the whole project team is risk literate and understands risk and the impact it has on the project
> - decision making includes a discussion of upside and downside risk
> - this project has some Critical Friends to challenge its assumptions and decisions

Once you know what you're doing, setting up an appropriate risk framework doesn't take a long time. It's much more helpful than flushing it down the toilet and hoping that makes it go away. Remember to put on those glasses to distinguish between the villains and the good guys. You'll feel a whole lot better, with no more sick stomach, because you'll be in control and leading from the front.

If your team needs to skill up and become risk-literate, subscribe to the Ghanvey library to do the 3P Risk learning module. They will learn the essentials, test their knowledge through an assessment and apply the knowledge in an output activity. The Ghanvey library will also give the team access to dedicated learning modules across each of the Activity Domains, a series of masterclasses that go deeper into the 'how to' and training to become a Critical Friend. Check it out at: **3pda.com.au/ghanvey/**

Outcomes and Benefits Management

Outcomes and benefits (O&B) management is important because it reduces the risk of a project falling off the rails. The project team should be checking in regularly, (e.g., annually on a 4-year roll-out) with progress against outcomes and benefits, because this can identify underlying problems and test strategic alignment. Good O&B management reinforces a consistent and logical approach to project implementation that improves the likelihood of success.

It's easy enough to lose sight of the original goal of your 3P roll-out due to the busyness of 1001 small tasks. This makes a consistent approach across Activity Domains so important, because this method helps you check off the 'vital signs', including O&B management, and test the pulse of the roll-out.

Before I give you an overview about what you're looking for in good O&B management, let me point out the common reasons why teams find them tricky to track. Have a look at Box 14, below.

If the 'tricky to track' indicators resonate with you, you've got some work to do. If you're not sure if you have warm and fuzzy outcomes and benefits rather than crystal clear ones, go and ask a Critical Friend to give you feedback and be willing to hear the answer. Have a close look at the data you're collecting, while you're at it. So much data is collected that is simply not relevant. It takes time to collect and report on, and your time to read it. Time is the key commodity that no one can afford to waste, so please think before you act.

Box 14: Indicators of tricky-to-track outcomes and benefits

- the statement of outcomes is a bit vague (i.e., warm and fuzzy rather than crystal clear)
- the desired benefits anticipated from the outcomes are not listed or are unclear (another warm and fuzzy job)
- the outcomes and benefits are not linked to (organisational) strategic outcomes
- mechanisms for collecting performance data are not in place or are unrealistic and there are no plans for evaluating the impact of the project
- the project team and/or steering committee is not confident the activities will result in meeting the desired outcomes

A project I worked with in the health sector some years ago was in a desperate state when the team called me. They were a government funded program, and they'd had a call out of the blue from their contract manager to say they would no longer be funded. The new government contract manager couldn't figure out what the government was getting for its investment and had decided to call it quits. "We've submitted all our reports," the program manager told me. "I just don't understand what the problem is. We work really hard and our program is very important."

After looking through all the reports they had submitted over eight years, I identified two key problems. The Service Agreement and the report template were poorly designed. The Service Agreement wrapped up the purpose and outcome into one broad statement like: 'Collect samples for research.' Benefits weren't part of the equation. The Key Performance Indicators (KPIs) were around collecting samples and having meetings. They were so broad that they weren't measuring anything in particular.

On the program side, the organisation had been around for eight years, collecting a lot of clinical samples from hospital patients for research, as per their desired outcomes and KPIs. They didn't know when to stop. They had just continued collecting. They couldn't tell anyone how many samples they had or for what particular disease streams. They also couldn't say with any confidence how many researchers had used their samples, or to what end. They were good people who were very smart and committed to their good work, they just had no way of showing anyone else why that work was important, or how that work made a difference.

Let's leave our friends here and come back to them later when we have a look at what good O&B management looks like and how it can help turn things around. Just before we go, I want you to be clear on the moral of this story. Without a clear outcome, you're running a high-risk operation, because you're not aiming to achieve anything in particular. Everyone is very busy and doing good work, the sort of work that will ultimately make your funder resent you.

Proactive O&B management provides a clear guide to everyone involved with the project that this is the goal, the reason why you're doing those 1001 small tasks. When O&B performance is clear and tracking well, it's easy to please funders and stakeholders alike. See Box 15 (below) for my top picks for healthy O&B indicators.

Box 15: Indicators of easy to please 3P outcomes and benefits management

- project goal is crystal clear, pithy (i.e., not more than 25 words) and written down

- anticipated benefits are identified and clear

- the outcomes and benefits are strategically aligned to the organisational strategy or policy

- appropriate data collection is in place and there are appropriate plans for evaluating the impact of the project

- the project team/steering committee and other key stakeholders are confident that current activities will lead to meeting the outcomes and desired benefits

I always find it useful to begin with a clear picture of what success looks like and discuss how that is different to now. A couple of simple questions can open up a whole lot of information you might not otherwise have tapped. Here is an example you can use in almost any social purpose setting. Think mental health reform, family violence reform, substance abuse initiative, you get the drill. You're going to need to flesh it out a bit more than dot points. I'm using dot points for convenience and brevity. This is a pretend reform program.

1. If we were successful at delivering the desired outcomes on our service reform program, what would that look like?
    - less duplication for clients and staff
    - a different way of organising our service offering
    - a different way of partnering with other organisations or services
    - skilled, confident and satisfied staff

2. If we were successful at delivering our desired outcome, what difference would it make?
   - our clients would be safe and have a higher rate of staying with the recovery program
   - our clients would be achieving better recovery outcomes
   - the service cost would be reduced, and we could serve more clients
   - our staff would be more satisfied because they are serving more clients effectively
   - the way we did things would be a 'showcase' for other similar organisations
   - organisations would be banging on our door to partner with us
   - our funders would have agreed to expand our program

It's time to revisit our friends from earlier who were about to lose their funding because no one could figure out what they were doing. These guys were very open and willing to do whatever it took, because they needed to keep the funding. They started by clarifying their purpose. Instead of stating 'collect samples for research', they refined this to: 'Collect samples of X disease for global research'. They backed this up with a clarifying outcomes statement, even though they were an ongoing program. They knew they needed something to work towards over the next five years. They decided, after some heated debate, that the primary outcome they were looking for was to have a world-class collection of annotated samples of X disease, with A–K sub streams that researchers could access within 48 hours of request.

This clearly articulated outcome focused their business model and their systems. The team set to work across every relevant area needed. They:

- got information out of their heads, where only they knew it, and onto paper where they could show real merit
- counted, cleaned, annotated and databased their samples and developed a protocol for future sample collection
- realised they were taking two weeks or more to get a requested sample to a researcher, so they invested in new IT systems to speed that up
- changed their business and governance model and their data reporting
- checked their progress each other month to make sure they didn't waste any of their precious time or resources with activities that weren't helping them get to their desired outcome
- mitigated their risk of income losses by connecting to multiple sources of revenue. These guys also connected to their researchers a lot more, so they could better understand the clinical development that happened as a result of using their samples

The benefits achieved were powerful, so they went on and developed some case studies to communicate that message to funders and other stakeholders.

This organisation was unrecognisable for all the right reasons, just 18 months after the wake-up call. I'm pleased to say their funding agency was also impressed and understood what value they were getting for their investment. The focus derived from setting a clear outcome was worth it: they got their money and were achieving outcomes and related benefits in clinical practice improvements that everyone understood.

Once again, let's just check in about the moral of the story. A warm and fuzzy outcome will have people working hard, doing their own thing, with their own idea of what the outcome is supposed to be. The outcome is never met because no one knows where the destination is and whether they've made it. The focus turns to the activities for their own sake, which leads them down the road to nowhere in particular and frustrates their funders.

On the other hand, a clear outcome statement focusses activity on a clear destination. It helps to prioritise resources and activities. If you organise your activities into the Activity Domains and track them across the Lifecycle phases, you'll soon pick up anyone who has taken a wrong turn and you'll be able to set them back on the right road before they go too far in the wrong direction.

Going off track is a huge and common waste of time, energy and resources. Please, please, please actively manage your outcomes and benefits by health checking your 3P roll-outs regularly. On a program or project of four years or more, the project team should call in some independent Critical Friends to conduct health checks annually. With a shorter project, check your progress towards desired outcomes twice annually. Many organisations have checks and balances that are not often used. Get them out of the cupboard and dust them off. Create a pool of internal Critical Friends to help each other and learn from each other. It's all about moving the project forward towards the desired outcome. Make it happen.

Chapter 4: Key Messages for the Activity Domains

1. **Governance** - understand the decisions that need to be made across the LifeCycle phases and establish a structure that facilitates decision making. Think lean.

2. **Financial Management** - identify how money will be allocated across each LifeCycle phase. Identify the connection of performance to financial allocation and identify how financial problems will be managed.

3. **Stakeholder Engagement and Communication** – understand your stakeholders and tailor engagement in a timely manner. Engage with authenticity.

4. **Capability Management** – acknowledge three layers: capable organisations learn from all projects; capable teams are social purpose project management literate; capable service providers are supported.

5. **Risk Management** - identify how you will manage compliance, and manage and respond to potential problems and facilitate opportunities. Develop a project risk register if needed. Educate staff to be risk literate.

6. **Outcomes and Benefits Management** - identify the evaluation framework. Identify KPIs and key data to be collected. Identify how you will track progress with implementation, outcomes and benefits realisation (i.e., annual 'health check', focus groups with program users, reporting arrangements).

CHAPTER 5

Ghanvey Method Critical Friends

Most of my clients are typical social policy and social community sector people, which means they are run off their feet trying to fit everything in. While they are smart and savvy, they are also way too close to their projects to objectively assess where they're up to.

Critical Friends are a pool of people the team has on call to help with objective assessment of a project's progress. They might be internal, from a different area (not working on this particular 3P roll-out), or external. Usually, a combination of both is a good place to land. Critical Friends should be familiar with your work but not close to it. They need to be experienced in successfully delivering strategic social purpose programs or projects and they need to be people you can trust.

"What do they do?" I hear you ask. Great question. Critical Friends look over your documentation and listen to your accounts of how things are going on the ground. They may even need to talk to some key stakeholders to hear their perspectives. The one or two Friends will then give feedback to you on any gaps they found that could impact the roll-out going forward. It is a quick, point-in-time stop to assess the future. It's not about auditing – leave that to the auditors. It's about making sure the project has the best possible chance of success. Sometimes, the gaps can be minor and quite easily fixed along the way. At other times, the gaps might be significant and will need to be fixed urgently before the roll-out can keep moving. You would be amazed at the sorts of gaps that can be found by a set of objective eyes.

Critical Friends should be called upon when it's time to transition to the next LifeCycle phase so they can help you objectively assess whether you're ready to move forward. If you have a Cruise phase longer than 12 months, then Critical Friends should be called upon to give a 'health check' assessment annually. You don't have to use all of them, all the time. That's why you build a pool of people, to spread the load. Identify your Critical Friend pool of people early in LifeCycle Phase One: Post-Budget Planning and confirm they are willing to play their part.

Other roles for Critical Friends can include providing support for solving wicked problems you may be facing or providing broader support for that 'team of one.' I can't guarantee Critical Friends will come to you *gratis* and that's why I encourage organisations to build an internal pool of Critical Friends. Having said that, it's always a good idea to have at least one external set of eyes providing independent oversight two or three times a year, as they can question the status quo in ways that internal eyes can't.

It is vital to call your Critical Friends in because you'll have to prepare for their visit. You'll want to start checking off the Activity Domains yourself and then you'll have to stop to hear what they have to say. They will probably only need a day or two, depending on the size and complexity of the 3P roll-out, but that time could save you months' worth of mistakes down the track. While it might not seem like it at the time, your Critical Friends are your 3P roll-out cheerleaders.

When I was working with a client a few years ago as a Critical Friend, they were crazy busy trying to roll-out a pretty big project in a very tight timeframe. Everyone on the team was smart, dedicated, moving fast and pushing ahead. Their head executive decided to do a 'health check' to test progress. The team did not want to stop. They were way too busy and were terrified that stopping for a few days to assess where they were up to would blow their timelines forever. The atmosphere was a little frosty when I went in, as staff made it clear I was a burden on their time. "Here you go, I think this is the latest version, but there might be another one. Anyway, you can access the drive to find anything you want. We're really busy. See how you go and call out if you need help."

To cut a long story short, this team could talk about what they were doing really well. However, their documentation was way behind because they didn't see the value in keeping it up to date. I discovered that two of the staff were looking for promotions and two others were very new and had come from outside the organisation. They were finding it difficult to catch up to the others because the documentation was so out of date and had sent them in the wrong direction, more often than not. Most of the critical information was inside the heads of the staff about to leave, and these people were almost impossible to access.

Apart from the gap between what the documentation said and what the staff said, (which could be fixed relatively easily), the project seemed to be rolling along well, until one particular interview.

"How are you going to do this really big chunk here? Isn't this the crux of the whole project that all your service providers are going to tap into?" I asked one of the new staff members.

"We're going to outsource that," she responded confidently, "but it isn't needed until almost the end of the year. We've got lots to do before then."

Mmmm, I thought, *that's only five months away*. "That's a pretty big job," I continued. "Do you need to go through a process for that?"

"Oh, yes, there's a system. I've only been here a couple of weeks, so I'll learn about that over time."

"I've done a lot of work with these organisations and I'm pretty sure the process takes about six months. I think you might have to book it in with the procurement team several months in advance."

"You're kidding me. Six months! That's a lifetime. I thought we could do it in about six weeks."

"Are you confident you could write up detailed specifications for something like this?"

"No way. It's really technical."

It turned out no one knew how to write specifications for a procurement like this, and no one had been directly involved in a significant procurement before. It was a massive capability gap. Everyone was so busy doing all the other bits, the procurement piece wasn't even on the radar, but it was about to derail the entire project. It was a massive risk.

The first moral of the story is that a fresh set of eyes can see what you can't. It's not because you're incompetent, it's because you're way too close to the project to be objective. Call in your Critical Friends to help you get the best out of your project. Yes, it can be confronting at times, but it's a good sort of confronting, because it gives you the best possible chance of success. You can train up a pool of internal Critical Friends when you subscribe to the Ghanvey library at the website: **3pda.com.au/ghanvey/**.

Of course, if you call on others to be your Critical Friends, you'll probably exchange your own goodwill and become a Critical Friend to them. This can be a structured organisational approach or an informal arrangement among teams. Whichever way, using this approach consistently builds capability, reduces risk and links you into a virtuous circle of continuous improvement.

Chapter 5: Key Messages

1. Critical Friends challenge assumptions, objectively assess project health and can help solve wicked problems.

2. Critical Friends can be internal (from outside the project team) or external. A combination of both works well.

CHAPTER 6
The Ghanvey Magnificent Matrix

All the business books I've read say you should never fall in love with your own ideas, but I'm afraid it's too late! I developed what I call The Ghanvey Magnificent Matrix and it's something I love with all my heart and soul. It does so much. It maps your 3P roll-outs in an organised way, it covers all the bases, and it can be used to quickly map critical decisions across the LifeCycles to help you determine the best-fit governance structure for a project. Finally, it turns into a perfect reporting tool for a project 'owner' or steering committee.

This is a short chapter to introduce you the Ghanvey Magnificent Matrix and how to use it. Part 3 of this book will then guide you how to apply the practice, with a range of activities that take you through the LifeCycle phases and the Activity Domains.

To see it all at once might overwhelm you, so let's build the Ghanvey Magnificent Matrix step by step.

Are you ready?

Step One – Project name

Whether they are at the start or partway through a 3P roll-out, I make all my clients name their project. It sounds simple, but you'd be surprised how many projects I've seen that are part of a bigger program and haven't named their own bit of it. The team is aware they are part of that bigger reform program, but they're not crystal clear about how exactly to describe their part of it. Naming your particular part of any bigger program or naming a standalone one is essential to getting clear about project boundaries and interdependencies.

PROJECT / PROGRAM NAME:

Step Two – Project success

Everyone needs to be clear about what success looks like. This is the goal and the reason why someone gave you money to change something. Lots of teams find this a bit tricky because they see success as the overall reform program success. While you definitely need to be aligned to the overall program or organisational goal, you still need to be able to describe what this particular slice of the pie is going to achieve. My very strong recommendation is to try and describe your program or project success in 25 words or less. Make it pithy and make it clear. This is the destination picture everyone should be able to look to in order to check if their actions are getting them there.

PROJECT / PROGRAM NAME:
SUCCESS IS:

Step Three – LifeCycle phases

Now we're clear about what this 3P roll-out is and what it's aiming to achieve, we can start looking at how to organise it in a way that will focus actions towards the goal. Step three is about the LifeCycle phases themselves. Strategic programs and initiatives have a predictable flow, from the time you receive the money to the time the funded period ends. It's just the same as any other program or project delivery.

The phase colours match the colours on the LifeCycle phase circles from Chapter 3. As a visual person, I find colours a useful way to identify almost anything. "Where's that Community Report?" I'll say. "You know, the one with the yellow cover?" For those of you who find the LifeCycle phase concept challenging, just focus on the colours. Ask yourself, "What do we need to do in the green phase?"

The rest of the chapters in this book are about the LifeCycle phases and will guide you through the sorts of actions that should go in each one. The Ghanvey Method also provides a guide about how you know when you're ready to move from one phase to the next.

Step Four – LifeCycle phase goal

Having an individual Phase Goal is important for keeping you focused and strategically aligned with the end goal. Without it, you can easily become trapped in the busyness of those 1001 tasks. With a Phase Goal, you can keep an eye on whether the actions you're taking are actually relevant to the Phase Goal you want to achieve, and consequently to the Project Goal. Once again, this might sound overly basic, but I've seen so many teams busy with actions that are simply not relevant to the project that I've decided it's a very important element to practice. I've included some broad phase goals in the example below, but you can choose your own if you'd prefer.

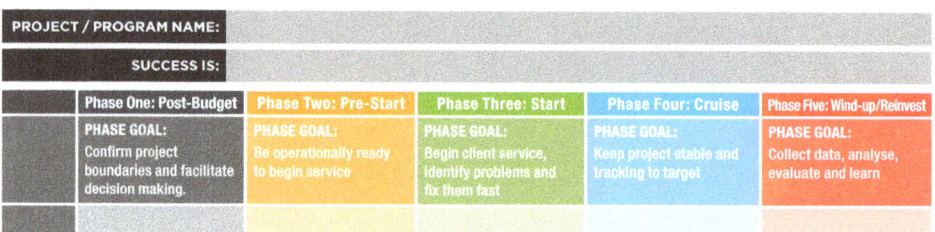

That's the top of the Ghanvey Magnificent Matrix covered, going from left to right. Now we'll sync it with the left side, going from top to bottom.

Step Five – The Ghanvey Magnificent Matrix

Isn't it just beautiful?! With consistent practice and application, you'll learn how to use it and it will never let you down.

The Ghanvey Magnificent Matrix is a great discussion guide for your team and a useful item to share with your Critical Friends as you plan your 3P roll-out. If you're a team of one, discuss it with your mentors. Begin your discussion by taking a LifeCycle phase — let's say LifeCycle phase one: Post-Budget planning — and ask yourself, "If we planned our roll-out, what would it look like?" Then, use the Activity Domains to guide the 'what' part of the plan. Your answers form the headline actions that appear in the relevant cell.

Ghanvey Magnificent Matrix

PROJECT / PROGRAM NAME:						
SUCCESS IS:						
Activity Domains	**Phase One: Post-Budget** PHASE GOAL: Confirm project boundaries and facilitate decision making	**Phase Two: Pre-Start** PHASE GOAL: Be operationally ready to begin service	**Phase Three: Start** PHASE GOAL: Begin client service. Identify problems and fix them fast	**Phase Four: Cruise** PHASE GOAL: Keep project stable and tracking to target	**Phase Five: Wind-up/Reinvest** PHASE GOAL: Collect data, analyse, evaluate and learn
Governance					
Financial Management					
Stakeholder Engagement					
Capability Management					
Risk Management					
Outcomes & Benefits Management					

Once you've mapped out the headline actions needed, you can add a timeline across the bottom of the Matrix. The timeline will provide a context for the resources needed to achieve the outcome (i.e., to get the actions done in time). The combination of illustrating actions needed across a specific timeline might even help to support a case for additional resources to bring a realistic picture of alignment to the two, if needed.

Here's a brief example. We're filling in LifeCycle Phase One for a strategic reform program. If we ask, "If we planned our roll-out, what would it look like?", the answer would include the following items against each of the Activity Domains:

1. *Governance* plan that confirms a clear governance structure (i.e., one that facilitates decision-making) and identification of Critical Friends.
2. *Financial allocation* plan that tracks allocation across each of the Lifecycle phases and includes what to do with financial problems.
3. *Stakeholder engagement and communication* plan that separates stakeholders into different categories and includes when they move from foreground to background and vice versa along the roll-out journey (across each LifeCycle phase).
4. *Capability* plan to ensure the organisation (or at least the team) is learning from the roll-out and the team always has the skills (or access to the skills) needed for each LifeCycle phase to proceed on time, and the service providers (if relevant) are capable.
5. *Risk* plan to comply with the law, prevent or mitigate threats and facilitate opportunities. This may include a risk register if needed.
6. *Outcomes and Benefits* plan including clear project objectives, an evaluation framework (even if it's very

small and informal), key performance measures, data collection and reporting confirmation.

Remember, plans are specific to the 3P roll-out and contain actions that will move you towards eventual achievement of the project goal.

You might not come up with all of this in one discussion session, indeed, you may need two or three team discussions. Keep these discussions tight, relevant and focused on the project purpose and outcome to get the best results. Then, of course, you have to pull together all the items. The length of time you need to do that will give you a sense of the duration timeline for the LifeCycle. As you're pulling the work together, I suggest you keep talking about it with your colleagues. When you deliberately name the actions that align with the dedicated Activity Domains, you and the team will be confident that all bases are covered.

You will have your own administrative ways of accessing and changing documents, however, just for the record, I'm a big believer in having one person 'own' the master copy of the Ghanvey Magnificent Matrix and be responsible for updating it after discussions. This is good practice for project management, so you don't get a situation where lots of different versions are floating about.

Some people ask me if it's okay to share the Ghanvey Magnificent Matrix with key stakeholders and Critical Friends. My answer is yes. It is particularly helpful to share the Ghanvey Magnificent Matrix with the people you or your team report to, and definitely with Critical Friends. A note of caution about sharing outside your key reporting stakeholders, though: stakeholders who are not familiar with the Ghanvey Magnificent Matrix may misinterpret how it works. Like any documentation shared more broadly among stakeholders, you need to make sure everyone accessing it understands what is before them and how they can get the best out of it.

Reporting to the executive or steering committee is going to be so much easier if you can tell them *exactly* where the project is up to in the context of a particular LifeCycle phase, and against each of the Activity Domains. It's even better if you can show them what the Critical Friends think about the progress that's been made. Executives and steering committees will love you because anyone who can simplify reporting for very busy people to help them get across if quickly is always a shining light.

I hope I've made it clear that the Ghanvey Magnificent Matrix is a living and breathing tool that stays with you for the duration of your 3P roll-out journey. Once you've plotted your course towards success, you'll have to be realistic about whether you're ready to move to the next LifeCycle phase. This is no slap-dash, "We're fine, we just have to keep moving," type of exercise. You'll need to consider where the Activity Domain actions are up to, whether they continue to be relevant to the project goal and whether everything is still aligned.

Moving ahead when only part of a LifeCycle phase is complete is a recipe for disaster. Do you really want to leave that risk plan sitting on the shelf? If you said "yes," you need a holiday. The right answer is "no." As you enter each new LifeCycle phase, it is an opportunity to refresh all your plans so they remain relevant to any changes in the wider environment that might impact the roll-out. This is also the time when Critical Friends come in to help.

In the Ghanvey Method, you (and your Critical Friends) check progress against each Activity Domain towards the end of each LifeCycle phase, in preparation to transition to the next phase. It helps facilitate a smooth transition and a smoother ride through the new phase. It forces you to momentarily stop and think ahead. You'll have to consider the different skills you need and the shifts in stakeholder engagement you require. You'll be forced to confront the unspent money that is piling up, and the additional risks imposed by that leadership change. It's also time to have a look at the data you've got so far and consider what it's telling you. In other words, this momentary pause prepares you to take the action you need to go forward confidently.

Conclusion

In my experience, successful 3P roll-outs do not happen by coincidence. They happen because the responsible team has a method that is consistently applied and well understood by everyone around them. The team can name project financial or risk indicators confidently. They understand the changing roles of the same stakeholders across the roll-out journey. They know the end game and can tell if an activity is relevant to it or not. Consistency builds competency, which ultimately brings success. The Ghanvey Method works, and, if applied effectively, will mitigate risk and amplify outcomes every time. Organisations wanting to invest in success can subscribe to the Ghanvey library of dedicated learning modules, masterclasses and Critical Friend training at the website: **3pda.com.au/ghanvey/**.

Chapter 6: Key Messages

1. The Ghanvey Magnificent Matrix brings together the LifeCycle phases and the Activity Domains.

2. The Ghanvey Magnificent Matrix has five steps:
- step one: project name
- step two: project success
- step three: LifeCycle phases
- step four: LifeCycle phase goals
- step five: the Ghanvey Magnificent Matrix

3. The Ghanvey Magnificent Matrix has multiple uses, including:
- planning the entire roll-out
- decision mapping
- reporting
- Critical Friend health checking.

Working the Ghanvey® Method

Introduction

In my research for this book, I came across a book by Will Gompertz, BBC Arts Editor, called *Think Like an Artist* (2015). I love learning from different sectors; it's so liberating. In describing the creative process, Gompertz crystallised the point I was trying to convey about planning for a 3P roll-out as being one "Simple but demanding rule: always think both big picture and fine detail." (Gompertz 2015, p.116)

If you think about the LifeCycle phases as being part of the big picture and the Activity Domains as the detail, it can make it a lot easier to understand how it all fits together.

Gompertz's description of how the creative process works (when it is done well), parallels the LifeCycle approach to planning 3P roll-outs. Gompertz sums it up perfectly when he reflects that:

"It [the creative process] requires your mind to constantly go back and forth, one moment concerned with the minutiae, the next stepping away and seeing the broader context. Spend too much time on the fine detail and you will get lost. But if you only think about the big picture you won't create or connect to anything. The two have to work together in sync. If they separate, disaster strikes." (Gompertz 2015, p.119)

If you manage your 3P actions in the Activity Domains and across the LifeCycle phases, you'll be able to synchronise the big picture with the details.

I encourage clients to practice using the Ghanvey method on smaller projects, at first. That way, you can build confidence and competence when the stakes are not so high. You'll soon notice an authentic transformation taking place that is reducing risk and amplifying outcomes like you've never seen them before.

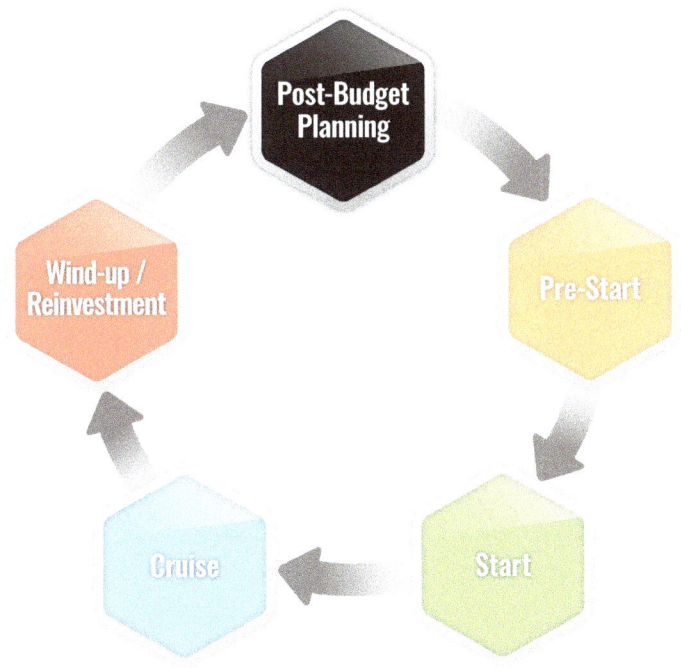

CHAPTER 7

Ghanvey LifeCycle Phase One:
Post-Budget Planning

Introduction

The Ghanvey method for 3P roll-outs begins with budget confirmation. This is usually prior to the start of your financial year, albeit sometimes only by weeks. Regardless of whether you get eight weeks' or three weeks' notice, you have to be ready to hit the planning accelerator immediately. The more you can achieve before the start of the financial year (the official start time for most 3P roll-outs), the better you will cope later.

The front-end of any 3P roll-out is intense, so following a method makes your time use much more effective. *Phase One: Post-Budget Planning* is about getting your house in order before starting to deliver the service. This phase is about gaining agreement from project 'owners' (such as an individual executive or a steering committee) about *how* you're going to get to your destination, *who* you need to come with you and *when* you will arrive. If ever there was a need to draw on the capability for synchronised big picture and detailed work, it is in this phase.

In this chapter, we're going to take a look at setting up a strong foundation for your 3P roll-out. This starts with repeating a couple of very important lessons from Chapter 2:

- implementation is about planning *and* doing
- consistency is the key to success

Once again, I'm going to bang on about using a consistent approach to your 3P roll-outs — the Ghanvey method — because it reduces risk and amplifies outcomes, every time.

The Fundamentals

If you're tasked with 3P roll-out oversight or you're the person tasked with implementation, then why not do it well? It takes less time and a lot less effort and, once you know what you're doing, it will help to reduce risk while amplifying outcomes.

Let's begin with repeating one of those points I want you to write down, remember and embed in your mind:

implementation is about planning *and* doing. So many people think implementation is just the doing bit. They think that if they're not 'doing', they're not implementing, and that makes them panic. Get that out of your head right now, because I'm telling you, with all of my 25 years' experience informing this understanding: **implementation is about planning *and* doing.** Planning is a legitimate part of doing, and it absolutely must come first if you want your 3P roll-out to succeed. Planning gets rid of the guesswork, which is where most of the risk lives.

One way of thinking about planning is like setting your Satellite Navigation (or 'Sat Nav') to take you to a desired destination. The Sat Nav can only take you there if you entered in parameters like a street name, number and suburb. In other words, it can't read your mind. If you feed the Sat Nav the wrong information, e.g., the wrong suburb, guess where you're going to end up? You guessed it, not where you desired to go, but where you programmed the Sat Nav to take you. If you want to get to the desired destination, you need to enter accurate parameters. This means you need an accurate set of parameters to start with, because Sat Navs don't do vague, "Maybe, I think that's right," kind of instructions. Sat Navs are set for success every time because they demand clarity from you *before* they start 'doing'.

Shrinking budgets for individual 3P roll-outs are increasingly common, so it's likely your pre-budget plans will need revision to reflect a reduced budget. In other words, you'll need to reset or confirm your destination. That will have flow-on effects for establishing your evaluation framework and success indicators, and even the way you measure those indicators.

One program that stands out for me requested $30 million over four years. They were in despair when their confirmed funding turned out to be $14 million. The funder didn't give any instructions about what to prioritise with the reduced dollars. The team didn't know what to do, and just started doing. You can guess what happened as they tried to implement a program that was designed to have more than double the money. It was total chaos and stress, and not a single element of the program was delivered well.

Like I said earlier, the planning part of implementation doesn't have to take excessive amounts of time, but it does have to be done if you want to reach your destination in the quickest, most effective way.

The Fundamental Drawing Board

If you're planning a program or project from scratch, practice caution and don't over-promise. Take these lessons to heart and try your very best to avoid them. When I was talking with a range of 3P professionals as part of the research for this book, some of them pointed to what they believed was a widespread problem: promising to deliver the world on a shoestring budget. "So many social project and program planners feel that if they don't promise the world, they won't be considered legitimate," they told me.

Promising the world when you only have the budget, skills and overall capability to deliver a small suburb will strike you off the legitimate list in no time at all. It's a recipe for disaster and doesn't serve anyone well. Funders might jump for joy at the thought of getting a bargain, but they will soon resent you when you flounder and fail. Let me repeat again: it is far better to do a small program or project offering and do it well. Please learn this lesson, otherwise you're putting in time, energy and money, for nothing – literally.

Here is the awful truth: if you try to stretch your program too far, it will always undermine your ability to reach desired outcomes. If you find yourself in this position, explain to stakeholders what happened and what it means for what you can do. They probably won't be happy, but they'll be more likely to respect you and work with you to lift the quality of what's in front of them. It's also going to be very hard to evaluate a 3P roll-out that is not contained to a rigorous boundary. This, in turn, makes it hard to demonstrate that you achieved something. If you can't demonstrate that you achieved something, it's going to be increasingly difficult to attract more funding.

Learning from these sorts of painful scenarios is very important. Try to develop relationships with your funding partners to better understand the costing evidence they are looking for. Use the LifeCycle phasing approach in your proposals to help funders better understand how this 3P roll-out will work. Finally, face the harsh choices and don't promise what you simply can't achieve. No one wins if you do that.

The key to a disciplined approach for making effective choices is to stop fixating on constraints, no matter how systemic they may appear to be. "We can't do that because…" is a bad habit and can easily become a way of life in teams and organisations, if it's not checked. At the end of the day, it boils down into a negative way of thinking that can cloud your vision and turn your focus towards what you can't do. Flip the focus to what you can achieve, instead. Making this shift returns your focus to where it should be: on your purpose, first principles, outcomes and specific objectives.

Reality re-set

"I can't revisit the 3P roll-out fundamentals," I hear you say, "because our program has been publicly announced. We have to do all of it, even though we didn't get the money we asked for and need." That would have to be the world's worst problem. The sense of doom is present from the outset, and while you continue to try your best, you know as well as any other 3P professional that failure is inevitable. Your chest tightens and your breathing gets shorter. Thoughts of finding another job come to mind, but things have already started to move quickly, so you just gather yourself up and jump in with the rest of them. Yes, I've been there, I get it.

I hear you when you say, "I don't have a choice." When it's already a done deal, going ahead regardless of budget reality seems like the only path. It's not. You can open up your possibilities and mitigate some of the pain by re-setting your 'how' piece (either from scratch or revised) through the Ghanvey Magnificent Matrix. Map out how the new budget reality plays out. Have a discussion around some key questions:

- What is the primary goal now?
- What happens in each of the LifeCycle phases now? Sift the actions into the Activity Domains
- Do we need our stakeholders to play a changed role? If so, what does that look like?
- Have the skills we need changed because we've had to prioritise some project elements and park others?
- What are our biggest threats and how do we mitigate them?
- What are the upside risk opportunities we could harness?

- How will we manage our financial allocation to make sure every cent is applied to achieving the project goal and not left sitting unspent because of a few trailing service providers?

Using the Ghanvey Magnificent Matrix in this way can support a reset of resources and bring a renewed focus on actions to make sure they're relevant to reaching your desired outcome. There's no room for time, energy or money to be spent on actions that are not going to get you closer to that goal. This means that the discussion will also need to include decisions about what you need to stop doing. The team will need to be realistic about this. If your part happens to be the bit that needs to be let go, then of course you'll be happy, because that's what will be best for the project (i.e., it's not about you). If you're flexible and adaptable, there will always be plenty to do, so you can switch to supporting the project in a different way while still being involved.

The Pithy Purpose

I have seen purpose statements on 3P roll-outs take up half a page or more, but still leave me none the wiser about what they hope to achieve. You can convey everything you need in 25 words or less.

Let's choose 'safe housing' as our example. Now it's time to define the overall purpose for this project in 25 words or less:

> To provide 100 safe houses, for victims of family violence and their children, statewide, by June 2025.

The purpose doesn't need to include the detail about whether houses are new or leased, the formula for geographic allocation of the houses, or the method of client triage, because all of that comes later. Just keep it clear and simple, so everyone involved in the project can stay focused.

Your turn:

> **ACTIVITY**
> Define your 3P roll-out purpose in 25 words or less.

Setting Scope

Setting boundaries around your project is absolutely critical to your ultimate success. There are many different ways you can go about this, and some of them are very sophisticated but can overcomplicate things, in my opinion. For me, it's all about simplicity and clarity. 3P scope can be beautifully defined by being crystal clear on the five Ws:

1. Why.
2. Who.
3. What.
4. Where.
5. When.

You'll also need to anticipate stakeholder interpretation by stating explicitly what is *outside* the boundaries you have set.

Setting your scope clearly is going to be even more important if you are re-scoping a 3P roll-out for a changed budget reality. Stakeholders who might have anticipated a role based on the original plans may no longer be needed, or at least not needed in the same way or to the same degree. They need to understand and prepare for the revised role they will play. Once again, stakeholders may not be entirely happy about the limitations you impose, but at least they will be clear.

Without a clear boundary, you can be vulnerable to scope creep, which is really just another name for a slow and painful death. Scope creep is when bits and pieces get added to your roll-out. They can seem inconsequential at first, and may be, if considered on their own. However, when considered collectively, they can break a project, because they nearly always rely on your existing resources to resolve.

If you don't have a clearly defined boundary that defines what's inside and outside (given the project goals and resources), additional bits and pieces can attach themselves to your scope surreptitiously. You might invite them knowingly or unknowingly or find them hard to resist if they're directly handed to you. Most of the time, I find they simply slip through the proverbial back door, and no one ever seems to know exactly how these elements became part of the project.

An overall impression of what your project is (but not a clear definition) won't be good enough to get you out of trouble. Even a somewhat clear impression means you and your stakeholders will be confused. Stakeholders may even believe they have a role to play when they don't. Even worse, they may start to act on that belief and cause serious headaches. Scope creep is a hugely common problem for 3P roll-outs, and if you want to succeed, you need to understand it and prevent it.

I'm a fan of pithy statements: short, sharp and simple. Everyone should be able to read them quickly and understand them easily. My favourite ones for these exercises include dot points, because they force clarity.

ACTIVITY

Using the guide below, write down the five Ws for your 3P roll-out.

1. **Why (rationale)** – this is designed to give your stakeholders context about why you are pursuing this particular project. For example:
   - *X Report illustrated the huge problem of victims of family violence needing accommodation and recommended 100 additional safe houses across the state*
   - *X Policy commits to provide 100 safe houses by X date, to be used by victims of family violence for up to 6 months, upon recommendation by police or a relevant service provider*
   - *Funding for the project is $X over four years*

2. **Who (stakeholders/partners/collaborators)** – this needs to outline who will join you in implementation and who will participate in the program/project. For example:
   - *X cohort of stakeholders will be in, Y cohort of stakeholders will not be included in this project (the definition of each stakeholder role is in a separate stakeholder engagement plan)*
   - *X cohort of clients will be in, Y cohort of clients will not be included on this project*

3. **What (activity streams)** – this outlines the key sub-streams of activity needed to achieve the purpose. The activity streams will match directly to your objectives. For example:

Ghanvey LifeCycle Phase One  *Post-Budget Planning*

- *Based on demand analysis from X report and focus group testing with relevant service providers, activity streams for this project will include:*
  - *Build 70 new stock*
  - *Lease 30 new stock*
  - *Establish statewide stock availability register for relevant services to access*
  - *Establish wrap-around services for tenants*
- *To allay concerns for some stakeholders, who may not even be directly involved with your project, you may need to add what is not being considered. For example:*
  - *This project will not be considering repurposing existing social housing.*

4. **Where (geography)** – this outlines where the activity streams will take place. For example:
   - *This project is statewide*
     - *Priority for housing will be given to areas of high demand, based on analysis from X report and on focus group feedback from service providers*
     - *Wrap-around services will be determined on geographic availability and common assessment priority tools, in consultation with service providers*

5. **When (timelines)**. For example:
   - *This is a four-year project ending in June 2025, and there is currently no commitment beyond this timeframe. Timing framework is as follows:*
     - *Phase One – Post-Budget Planning – May to June 2020*
     - *Phase Two – Pre-Start Readiness – July to August 2020*

- *Phase Three – Start and Test – Sept 2020 to Jun 2021*
- *Phase Four – Cruise – July 2021 to June 2025*
- *Phase Five – Wind-up/Reinvestment – July 2024 to June 2025*

SMART Objectives

Objectives for your 3P roll-out should relate directly to your activity streams and should sum up the deliverable for each stream. This helps to guide everyone working on a particular stream, so they understand what they are working towards. It may sound foolish in theory, but, in practice, it is very easy to get lost along the way in a crowd of busyness. One more thing to remember is to make sure your objectives align with your overall 3P roll-out purpose. You'd be surprised how many times this seemingly obvious step is overlooked.

> **ACTIVITY**
> Using the SMART guide below, define the objectives for your own 3P roll-out.

SMART Objectives (Specific, Measurable, Achievable, Relevant and Time-bound) are very helpful because they directly feed your need for clarity and simplicity.

For example: activity stream – safe house availability register

- *Specific* – the objective is to enable relevant service providers real-time information about safe house availability and location and enable them to reserve an available place for a client

Ghanvey LifeCycle Phase One Post-Budget Planning

- *Measurable* – measures are established around: real-time information; reliability; service access; service user confidence levels

- *Achievable* – resources needed to make this happen are: IT systems; trained staff; testing; $X

- *Relevant* – achieving this objective will improve access to safe houses, relieve pressure on the service system from double-handling clients and will make clients safe, faster

- *Time-Bound* – The register will be active by March 2025. Agile approach: initial testing at 3 months, revision where needed, test again at 3 months, revision where needed, test again at 3 months, then Cruise

Each sub-stream of a larger program or project can have its own Ghanvey Magnificent Matrix. This allows you to map decisions, plan actions against the Activity Domains, track progress and report against the Activity Domains for the sub-stream. That sub-stream will also need Critical Friends to check the project's health at the end of each LifeCycle phase. Just like the overall project Matrix, you can share the sub-stream Matrix with your key stakeholders. Just like the overall Matrix, you should only share if the stakeholders are familiar with what it is and how to interpret it.

I meant it when I said Phase One is intense! This is hard work, and you'll have to put in a few structured, two-hour sessions with the right people to get through the process of confirming your fundamentals in the context of your budget reality. Trust me, it is worth every uncomfortable debate, because everyone starting on the same page and understanding what the destination is means you're almost halfway to achieving outcomes success, already.

Now, let me explain how things can go wrong when you don't put all the pieces in place on your 3P roll-out. I supported a team a few years ago who were victims of their own success. Their role was to connect disadvantaged people to particular specialist services to help them begin to see, plan and have a stable future. It was an innovation program, and they had some early wins. They were working from an overarching government policy, flowing through to a high-level strategy.

"So, where's the pain coming from?" I asked.

"Well, we started out with a goal to support 500 participants, but now, just eight months in, that has grown to 1,500 participants." The problem was that they were working with one impression of the project, but their funding stakeholders had a different understanding of the project boundaries. Seeing the early success, these critical stakeholders had started to add all manner of 'plug-ins' to the core project. The reason this team called me was because they were terrified that they were about to be landed with a further 1,500 participants in the coming weeks and they couldn't figure out how to prevent this happening.

After retrofitting some defining features for this team, including a clear project name, a pithy purpose, a statement of scope and SMART objectives, we worked through the Ghanvey Magnificent Matrix. This allowed us to demonstrate what the team was doing and where they were up to. Armed with this new batch of clearly defined statements, the team felt they could proactively push back, and they did. They clearly communicated to the funding stakeholder about the boundaries of this project, including how the committed resources had already been fully allocated. They also provided a solution for what to do about the additional

1,500 cohort. It seemed to do the trick, and the team learnt their lesson. They would start on the front foot in future.

Going back to the proverbial drawing board to revise the fundamentals can seem like a time-consuming bore but I can assure you, it saves an enormous amount of time and effort down the track.

Now that you have the fundamentals sorted, you can move onto the other part of Phase One, which is planning for sustainable success.

Setting up Sustainable Success

Let's start with a reminder of the LifeCycle phases and the Activity Domains, because we're about to bring them together.

LifeCycle Phases and Activity Domains

Now that you've confirmed all the fundamentals, implementation moves onto planning actions across the LifeCycle phases. Actions fall under the six standard Activity Domains. These are used regardless of project content. You might be rolling out a grants program for supporting people with a disability to enter employment or investing in a longer-term program that supports young people at risk of alcohol and substance abuse. Maybe you're responding to practice reform after a Judicial Inquiry or Royal Commission or planning a significant change for your organisation. The Ghanvey method will apply in all of these contexts.

During Phase One, you're planning out what needs to happen across the entire LifeCycle of the 3P roll-out. It's more like a mapping exercise, as you consider what is needed across each different phase, in each separate Activity Domain.

Let's work through an overview of the sorts of things you might consider in the Activity Domains during Phase One mapping. I won't go over all the Activity Domains, because the repetition might put you to sleep. Instead, I'll zoom in on Governance, because Phase One is crucial to governance.

Governance

Governance is about the authorising structure for decision-making and about guiding the 3P roll-out through the LifeCycle phases to reach the destination on time, within allocated resources and with outcomes achieved. In other words, governance is the engine driving your implementation, so it's important to get a fit-for-purpose engine. It is common for organisations to automatically throw everything at the structure and super-size it. Steering committees, advisory bodies, project control groups – you name it, they'll have it. And then, they have a spaghetti chart to illustrate their governance structure, but no one really understands it and most people avoid it. If it's all too hard to manage, it won't be managed. So, what's the moral of the story? Keep the 3P governance framework lean.

There are three key elements to choosing your fit-for-purpose 3P governance framework:

1. Decision-making
2. Structure
3. Smart documenting

Decision-making

To keep your 3P roll-out moving forward, reflect on the sorts of decisions you need to make across the LifeCycle. Are they mostly everyday decisions, or is there a spattering of big stuff in there as well? If you're a one-person team rolling out a relatively small innovation project, you may be able tap into existing structures to authorise one-off big decisions, like a high dollar-value procurement.

On the other hand, if you are managing or are part of a team of three or more, and your project is in response to whole-of-sector reform (e.g., for mental health services), you'll likely have a lot of stakeholders who need to be involved in decision-making. You'll probably need to recruit people, and you may also have a large procurement in there that supports better coordination of services going forward.

ACTIVITY
Use the Magnificent Matrix to map out decisions needed in your own 3P roll-out.

Take a moment to reflect on the sorts of decisions you need to make in your own 3P roll-out. If you're near the start of your 3P roll-out, you might not know all the decisions that will need to be made, but you'll be across most of them, so work with what you know. Go to the Ghanvey Magnificent Matrix and quickly dot point the key types of decisions needed for each Activity Domain, in each LifeCycle phase. You can also try to put the big decisions, like the ones that need to go above the project team for authorisation, in bold.

ACTIVITY - 3P Decision-Making Matrix

Activity Domains	Phase One: Post-Budget	Phase Two: Pre-Start	Phase Three: Start	Phase Four: Cruise	Phase Five: Wind-up/Reinvest
Governance	• Scope / Objectives	• Authorise partnership agt			
Financial Management		• Tender process	• IT purchase • Training		• Allocating slippage
Stakeholder Engagement			• Stakeholder forum		• Focus groups
Capability Management	• Agree Capability needs	• Staff / Contractors • Training	• Volunteers	• Technical expertise	
Risk Management	• Agree Risks			• Agree risk mitigation	
Outcomes & Benefits Management	• Agree success measures	• Agree evaluation framework			• Evaluation and reporting

When you've done that, stand back and analyse what it throws up. Here are some questions you can ask yourself, as a guide:

Ghanvey LifeCycle Phase One  Post-Budget Planning

a) Are they mostly everyday decisions, about things like recruitment, or about purchasing small IT equipment and some other project-specific consumables?
b) How many decisions need to go above the project team for authorisation?
c) Which Activity Domains have the big decisions in them?
d) Do big decisions cluster in a particular LifeCycle phase?

Once you know the answers to these questions, you can start preparing to make them happen. The governance structure will be a key part of that preparation.

Structure

Once you're clear about the sorts of decisions you need to make, the structure follows. I caution clients about setting up too many committees. Like I said earlier, you're not there to host a dance party, you're there to guide this 3P roll-out towards its destination. The 3P governance structure must facilitate decision-making. The more layers you put in, the harder it is to get the decisions you need to keep the project moving forward.

Project structure should always be outcomes-focused.

Committees take an enormous amount of time to service. You have to do a lot of paperwork to set them up, write the Terms of Reference, coordinate diaries, set up meetings, write dedicated papers, prepare a presentation about the papers in case some members don't read the papers, circulate minutes and prevent factions forming around the table.

So, what's the moral of the story? Think lean for your 3P structure. Think outcomes-focused for your 3P structure.

If you really do need some committees, think about the way they facilitate decision-making. For example, if you need a sign-off for procurement specifications, but the authority to do that rests with a steering committee that only meets every other month, that's going to take too long. Make sure those sorts of things can be signed off within two to four weeks. If it's any longer, the structure is suffocating the project.

Committees come in many shapes and sizes, which is appropriate, because projects do too. Here's a reminder of some common committees used across 3P roll-outs and their purpose. There is a bit of flexibility about how these committees are formed and how they are used, however, the dot points below cover what happens in a wide range of 3P roll-outs.

Steering Committee

- usually comprises senior leaders, the project 'owners' or partners
- guides and steers the roll-out across the LifeCycle phases to success
- makes all the key project decisions and authorises plans for how you're going to do the project – that's your Activity Domains plans
- monitors and tracks project success, including outcomes and benefits realisation

Project Control Group

- usually used for each project sitting under an umbrella program
- usually comprises senior leaders of the project areas and should include one member of the steering committee

- monitors effective implementation of the particular project stream
- monitors interdependencies with other projects under the common program
- can be authorised to make decisions about integration and how interdependencies work on the ground

Working Group

- usually comprises representatives of the service providers or sector that is the subject of the 3P roll-out
- can give advice to the steering committee but does not make project decisions
- can also be used to share best practice among service providers
- usually continues for the duration of the project

Expert Advisory Committee

- fills in gaps of expertise that are needed at a particular time of the roll-out, but not all the time
- can be useful for harnessing stakeholder input
- signals that you value your stakeholders and don't want to take up too much of their time unnecessarily
- can provide advice to the steering committee or the project control group but is not a decision-making body
- usually comprises one member of the steering committee and/or project control group and experts

Finance / Audit / Risk Committee

- usually on larger projects to monitor resource allocation, risk and significant milestones
- may be applied to sub-streams of larger projects

- provides advice to the steering committee but does not make project decisions
- usually comprises at least one member of the steering committee along with two or three others who have relevant expertise

Remember, you don't have to have one of each to be impressive. Pick and choose what you need to keep your 3P roll-out rolling. If you're launching into a mental health reform program, you may well need one of each because there will be lots of partners and interdependencies, but if you're rolling out a single innovation project, you might only have a working group.

Once you've decided on the committees you might need, you have to be really clear on who is doing which role. Sometimes reporting lines for a 3P roll-out can be a little different to everyday reporting lines, so make sure key roles are allocated early.

Let's do a quick refresh on the distinction between accountability and responsibility.

Accountability is about who takes the rap for the success or failure of this 3P roll-out. It's not the same person who is *responsible* for everyday operations. The accountability 'owner' should be internal to the organisation, named and someone who can actively commit to owning accountability for this 3P roll-out.

The accountability owner is usually a senior-level person who has experience and can provide objective advice along the way. This person might chair the steering committee or be a senior-level executive who is not too close to the roll-out so can maintain objectivity accordingly.

Responsibility is allocated for everyday operational matters and for decision-making. A manager or coordinator is usually *responsible* for the everyday operations, even if they don't carry the authority for all of the decision-making. It is their responsibility to navigate the appropriate authorisations. For example, a manager might have the operational responsibility of tendering for services, however the authority for that decision may rest with a higher-level executive, depending on the financial controls in the organisation.

If you are the person assigned to figure out the governance structure, start with your 3P roll-out purpose and remember that governance is the engine driving implementation. Once you've got a draft structure, test a decision on paper and see how many steps it takes, up and down, to get an answer translated into action. Any more than four steps up and four back means that momentum will be in slow motion.

Any 3P roll-out moving forward in slow motion is annoying, frustrating, lacking in articulation and ultimately lacking in meaning. The only fast thing that comes out of it is the speed at which stakeholders lose interest.

The moral of the story is that your governance structure has a massive impact on your ultimate success.

Smart Documentation

Let's be honest, almost everyone despises writing up documentation. It takes time, something you rarely have to spare, and it's often hard to find if you need it. I get it, I really do. Nevertheless, I need to guide you with all the force of a megaphone. Listen carefully: documentation is not an aside for when you have spare time. It is integral to the project.

If you are time-poor and think you are saving time by not focusing on documentation, because you know what you're doing in your head, it will always work against you. Not documenting is a high-risk choice that will go unnoticed until something blows up. For example, the steering committee might have made a decision to purchase a multi-million-dollar IT system for coordinating services. It turned out to be a dud. When the auditors come in, they discovered that the steering committee *Terms of Reference* were never ratified, so they actually had no authority to make that decision in the first place. Oops! There's a front-page headline that could have easily been prevented.

Simple and clear documentation that is communicated effectively to the stakeholders who need to use it is the smart way to round off your governance framework. It prevents the path of high risk and confusion by keeping all stakeholders on the same page. It helps you manage risk by forcing you to be clear. If your documentation is too complex, it won't be read, because you're always going to be engaging with equally busy people who need to get across information quickly.

I feel like I'm trying to make you swallow some bitter medicine, but believe me, good documentation has very clear benefits. I've outlined these in Box 1, below.

Box 1: Benefits of Smart Documentation

1. **Clarity of purpose** - simple and clear documentation keeps everyone on the same page.

2. **Continuity of service** - as people come and go from the team, the documentation guides newcomers so they understand what this project is, where it's up to and how to keep the 3P roll-out on track.

3. **Integrity of practice** – demonstrates a rationale for choosing a particular pathway.

4. **Compliance** – demonstrates transparency and informs authorities about how this project was conducted, e.g., the appropriate sign-off was provided for that major contract.

This is where those extraneous committees can really bite. Every committee or advisory body needs volumes of paper just to get the members confirmed and inducted. That's followed by *Terms of Reference* and then a regular meeting agenda, meeting minutes, dedicated papers, a presentation about the paper for anyone who didn't read the papers, and a multitude of emails in between. That's a lot to keep up with but keep up you must. That's why I caution clients to only establish a committee if it will add value to decision-making.

Despite the volume of documentation that confronts you, believe me when I say, "Documenting saves time," because it does save time in cleaning up the mess that happens without it! Regular updating (this might be monthly, quarterly, half-yearly, or annually) takes very little time, but if you leave it for too long, it's going to be so much harder and more time-consuming when you do get to it, and then you'll just put it off again. You'll get better and faster at documenting with practice, so be smart and start practicing. Pop that time slot in the diary for the team to stop and check. For that hour every month, put on some music, have some cake and do an update swot. Try being creative to make it fun.

When you're finished, make sure to remember to communicate with relevant stakeholders about any changes or new versions of documents they may already have and rely on.

Your Critical Friends will want to see all your project documentation when it comes to assessing your project's health before the transition to the next LifeCycle phase. If it's not up to date, that will be noted in their report. At least you'll then have an idea which documents you need to get the project up to date.

If you were sitting in the hot seat at a Judicial Inquiry, could you swear all your documentation was up to date? I'm guessing you said "no." Here's an activity to start bringing you back on track.

ACTIVITY
Choose two documents from your own 3P roll-out that you know need updating and give yourself two weeks to update them.

As a guide for this activity, here is a list of documents that I find are often out of date.

- Purpose
- Objectives
- Scope
- Committee / advisory body Terms of Reference – ratified
- Committee agenda

Ghanvey LifeCycle Phase One   Post-Budget Planning

- Committee minutes
- Policies, procedures (e.g., financial delegations, IT, HR)
- Decision-making authorisation
- Activity Domain plans

The Magnificent Matrix

After all that, what does the Governance box look like in the Ghanvey Magnificent Matrix during LifeCycle Phase One? Intense and very busy. These are not the sort of actions that can be done on the fly. That doesn't mean they can't be done quickly, but dedicated attention and focus is needed if you also have a need for speed. It's hard to believe so many teams skip this phase, when you take a look at how it establishes the foundation of the entire project.

PROJECT / PROGRAM NAME:	
SUCCESS IS:	

	Phase One: Post-Budget Planning
Activity Domains	**Phase Goal:** Confirm project boundaries and facilitate decision-making
Governance	Confirm 3P Governance framework and structure Confirm project scope and objectives Establish Steering Committee and confirm members Allocate key roles Ratify SC *Terms of Reference* Prepare Activity Domain plans Authorise Activity Domains plans Line up Critical Friends

Figure 1: Ghanvey Magnificent Matrix cut out – Phase One: Post-Budget Planning. Activity Domain - Governance

Your turn:

> **ACTIVITY**
> In the cut out below from the Ghanvey Magnificent Matrix, dot point the tasks you need to complete in Governance, during Phase One: Post Budget Planning.

PROJECT / PROGRAM NAME:	
SUCCESS IS:	

Activity Domains	Phase One: Post-Budget Planning
	Phase Goal: Confirm project boundaries and facilitate decision-making
Governance	

Transition

"How will we know if we're ready to move to the next phase?" I hear you ask. Great question. You call in your Critical Friends for a health check that determines if your phase one actions are finished and robust.

For example, in Phase Two: Pre-Start, you're going to be doing things like recruiting staff or hiring additional experts. If your Capability Plan for the project only says, "Two additional staff will be needed," then it's not ready. It should say, "One

Ghanvey LifeCycle Phase One 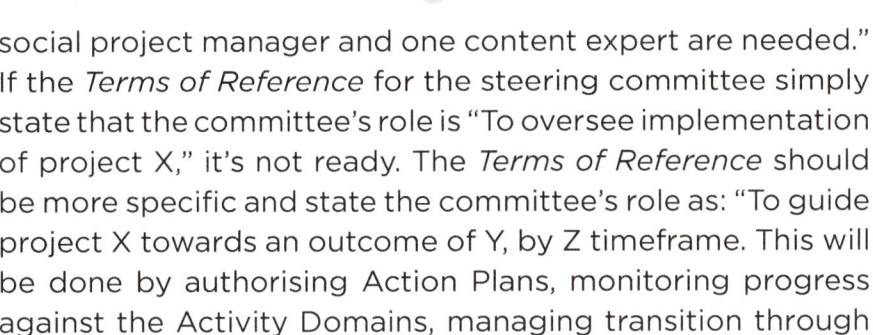 *Post-Budget Planning*

social project manager and one content expert are needed." If the *Terms of Reference* for the steering committee simply state that the committee's role is "To oversee implementation of project X," it's not ready. The *Terms of Reference* should be more specific and state the committee's role as: "To guide project X towards an outcome of Y, by Z timeframe. This will be done by authorising Action Plans, monitoring progress against the Activity Domains, managing transition through each LifeCycle phase and authorising financial decisions above $X amount." If I saw a statement like this, I would have confidence in the governance arrangements.

For a deep dive into each of the Activity Domains, you'll need to subscribe to the Ghanvey digital library where you and your team can access Critical Friend training, dedicated learning modules for each Activity Domain and a series of 'how-to' masterclasses: **3pda.com.au/ghanvey/**.

Even though this is early in the overall context of the 3P roll-out, you're already too close to make an objective assessment about your own work. Line up your Critical Friends early and let them help you. They can identify gaps and suggest ways to close them. Don't take it personally. Nobody's perfect. Expect a few gaps and be ready and willing to have a discussion that will ultimately improve your practice.

Conclusion

Phase One: Post-Budget Planning is a challenging and confronting phase to work through, especially if you're not in the habit of getting your house in order before you start a 3P roll-out. However, if you do this phase well, it will always be a win for you, your team and your desired outcomes.

The relative success of this phase will reflect the relative success of the entire roll-out. If you don't do it, you will fail (reality bites hard, folks). If you do part of it, you will be partly successful. If you do it all, you will be fully successful. The choice is yours.

Chapter 7: Key Messages

1. LifeCycle Phase One sets up the foundations of the entire 3P roll-out.

2. Implementation is planning *and* doing.

3. 3P scope can be defined by being crystal clear on the five Ws: why, who, what, where and when.

4. Consistency is the key to success.

5. Think lean governance structure. Think outcomes focused governance structure.

6. Smart documentation saves you time.

7. Stay close to the Ghanvey Magnificent Matrix. It's your best friend in a 3P roll-out.

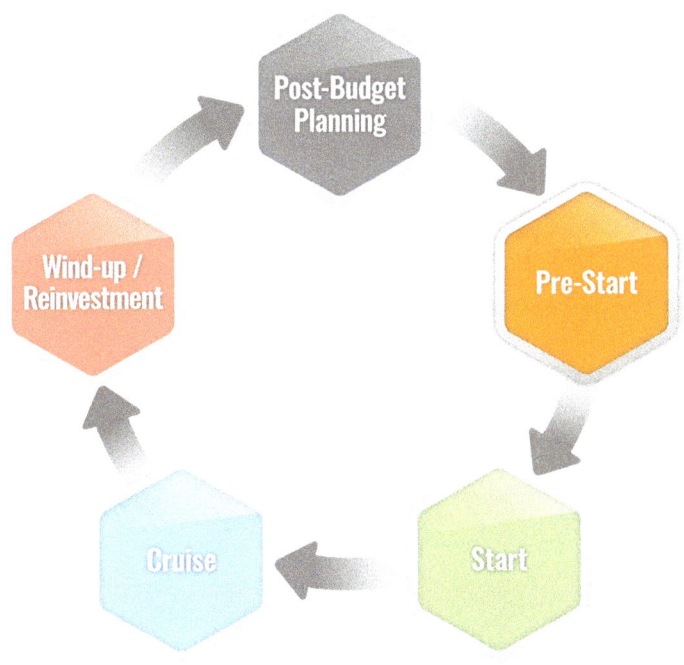

CHAPTER 8

Ghanvey LifeCycle Phase Two:
Pre-Start

Introduction

Before we get into the detail, let's recap where we're up to. So far, we've learnt about the concept of Social Project Management and the Ghanvey approach to this that brings together LifeCycle phases with Activity Domains in a way that is consistent and synchronised. We've also had a deep dive into LifeCycle Phase One: Post-Budget Planning, to better understand that implementation is about planning *and* doing. That's quite a lot to get your head around, but the hardest part is now behind you. The next four chapters focus on how best to sync the remaining LifeCycle phases with the Activity Domains.

The Pre-Start phase focuses on detailed actions across the six Activity Domains that need to happen *before* you can confidently 'open the doors' on day one. 'Opening the doors' can mean different things to different projects. It might be to start that grants program, begin the first actions on that reform program, or begin service delivery on that innovation project. If you happen to be applying the Ghanvey method more broadly, outside the social purpose sector, then your 'day one' might be entirely different again.

It is very important to bring these detailed actions to the foreground, because if you 'open the door' without stakeholders on the same page, with recruitment lagging behind and sub-optimal capability on the ground, you can guess what's going to happen. It's so predictable, and yet, it happens time and time again. The doors open to chaos and crisis, which inevitably come with a lot of added stress and risk, and it takes months for the project to streamline into the picture you originally envisaged.

If you do the Pre-Start phase well, you'll be able to open the doors confidently on day one and keep momentum moving towards the goal instead of dragging it forward, limping. As always, your Critical Friends will help you determine if you're ready to transition to the next phase. They'll be looking to see if the house is in order.

The big lesson in this chapter is to keep focused on the project goal, otherwise this phase could turn into a whole lot of busyness that begins to take on a life of its own, quite detached from the goal. This is where activities need to be monitored closely and streamlined across the Activity Domains to make sure they align with the goal. If you start heading off course so early in the project — and believe me this is a common problem — you're starting to waste resources. The time, energy and investment that is taking you in the wrong direction should be applied to working towards your goals. That's what efficiency is all about.

In this chapter, we will have a closer look at how four of the Activity Domains might look during LifeCycle Two: Pre-Start Phase, and I'll set up some activities so you can design your own Phase Two effectively.

1001 fiddly bits

Once you have finalised post-budget planning, you'll know what you need to do to open your proverbial doors on 'day one.' This phase is an important standalone phase that is about getting ready to hit the ground running for an effective start. Starting a project means being ready with all the people, systems, equipment, policies, delegations, compliance, committees, advisory bodies, contracts, partnership agreements and service agreements you need. It's about having these things signed off and ready to go and it also means making sure all service providers are ready to go as well.

Too often, the Pre-Start phase is combined with the Start phase. From my experience, this happens for two reasons. Firstly, it happens because most people don't recognise that getting ready to start is a distinctive phase that needs dedicated focus and attention. Secondly, I see that these phases are often combined because of time pressure. From where I sit, time pressure is often a disguise for lack of planning. So many times, I have arrived for an urgent project that "Has to start this week, and you'll have to do the work in-house," and the client doesn't have a desk or a computer for me, and I can't use anyone else's because I haven't yet been provisioned. It's not only incredibly annoying and makes me think this team is incompetent, it's also a big waste of time and money. Yes, I and all the other contractors and consultants in the universe can sit and read for a day or two, or even three. The most I've done is five days of reading on site, being told every day, "You should be provisioned later today." I'm pretty sure I was the only person on the floor who had read the 600 pages of the review. Is that really serving your objectives? "No," is the answer I hope I hear from you.

This sort of time wasting is rarely measured and evaluated, so it's hard to tell exactly how much impact it has, but I'm fairly certain it would be a lot of lost hours and money, if it was added up. What this tells me is that the team has already become lost in the process of starting and has not acknowledged the importance of the fiddly tasks that need to be done to facilitate an effective start that works. A team like this is not practicing efficiency.

There are plenty of time-consuming, fiddly tasks that need to be done prior to starting, and they need to be valued and acknowledged by management. Resist the urge to write this phase off as just 1001 little jobs that can be done in the background while attention and focus are on the 'real' game of starting. The truth is far from it. Phase Two: Pre-Start needs your focus just as much as the other phases. It is very much part of the 'real' game. It also needs a different skillset to Phase One: Post-Budget. Make sure you have someone in the team who thrives on detail (it won't be me) and let them lead you through it.

Ghanvey LifeCycle Phase One   Pre-Start   *Pre-Start*

There may be some crossover between LifeCycle Phase Two and Phase Three, however I advise caution about going to Phase Three (where delivery starts) before at least 80 percent of Phase Two is completed. Doing these sorts of activities well is valid and important work and will definitely progress the 3P roll-out in the right direction.

Working the Activity Domains in Phase Two

THE GHANVEY MAGNIFICENT MATRIX	
PROJECT / PROGRAM NAME:	
SUCCESS IS:	
	Phase Two: Pre-Start
Activity Domains	**Phase Goal:** Be operationally ready to begin service
Governance	
Financial Management	
Stakeholder Engagement	
Capability Management	
Risk Management	
Outcomes & Benefits Management	

Figure 1: Magnificent Matrix cut out of LifeCycle Phase Two: Pre-Start

Let's go to the six Activity Domains and have a closer look at some of them to illustrate what I'm talking about. I'll pull out a few common examples of where I see the biggest gaps for this phase.

Governance

Let's do a quick refresh on Governance before we continue. Governance comprises the systems, processes and structures needed to move implementation forward in a timely way that is appropriately inclusive, maintains integrity, is consistent with organisational values, complies with the law and achieves outcomes and benefits as intended.

In LifeCycle Phase One: Post-Budget Planning, the Governance phase was about establishing the foundational elements of the entire 3P roll-out, with a focus on decision-making, structure and smart documentation. In Phase Two: Pre-Start, the Governance phase has a shift in focus to bringing that structure to life. For example, it may involve seeking and appointing working group and advisory body members, ratifying *Terms of Reference* and/or authorising grants program criteria. It's not exactly exciting work for someone who likes visionary concepts and strategic planning, but others lap it up.

One of the most painful experiences of my public sector life was establishing a Ministerial Advisory Body. As you may know, the paperwork for these bodies is astonishing. It took weeks of to-ing and fro-ing to collect information from prospective members, and then one critical document wasn't signed, despite the 30 minutes on the phone that I'd spent talking through that exact form. We finally had a full package to send up to the Minister.

Ghanvey LifeCycle Phase One   Pre-Start

"We made it," announced our Office Manager, who had raced up the stairs to make the Friday cut-off. "Wohoo!" the rest of us cheered and had a little dance in our 'pod.' These were pre-COVID days when we were all office-bound. "Let's go for a drink," someone said, which we all agreed was a great idea. The relief was palpable on everyone's faces.

That weekend, there was a Ministerial re-shuffle. When we returned to the office on Monday morning, the Senior Policy Officer said to me "Do you think…?", trailing off because the words were too hard to say. "I think so," I said quietly.

The waiting was awful but mercifully short. By the afternoon, our executive came to our pod. "There's good news and bad news," he said. "The new Minister still wants this Advisory Body, but not these people." Handing me back the package we'd submitted on Friday night, he sighed in sympathy and said, "You'll have to start again."

For someone like me (who leans towards the big-picture thinking side of life), that re-shuffle was a total tragedy. I felt like bursting into tears. The thought of having to face all that paperwork again was completely overwhelming. However, being the team manager, I had to hold myself together. Fortunately, two other members of the team were loving it and just got on with the job, smiling. Right then, I loved those team members more than anybody else in the whole world. They knew they were the right people to lead the charge and they stepped up to the challenge. They were leading me, and I let them.

An important side note here: If you make a person who is a big-picture, strategic thinker do this sort of detailed planning, they will be very stressed and slow, and they won't do it well. Lots of the detail you need will be missed, and you'll be opening the door to compromised outcomes straight away. That strategic-minded person will try their best, but just they won't have the skills to do detail. It's rare to find someone who can do both – I'm talking 'less than 10 percent of the entire population' rare. Most of us lean towards one or the other. It's all about the way our brains are structured, but we're not going into that here.

A person who has the eye for detail and loves it is always going to be needed in the team and will be especially important during Phase Two: Pre-Start.

If you only have a one-person team, then allocate some dollars to provide that one person with support for the area they are not going to do well in. Yes, that means proactively and realistically anticipating human pitfalls. Learning preference assessments are a good way to determine a skill mix in any given team, and they usually come with self-awareness elements which can be helpful. When time and resources are pressing, I sometimes use a simple and very crude way of determining whether the one-person team is a big picture or detail person, by asking: "If you had a magic wand, what would your vision for this project be?" The big picture person will light up and start spouting ideas. The detail person will likely freeze and go blank.

The moral of the story is that it takes intense effort over weeks to close off those 1001 fiddly tasks, and this effort is a legitimate and essential part of the overall 3P roll-out LifeCycle. You simply won't reach your outcome goal without completing these tasks. This effort needs focused attention, specific capability, monitoring and support. If you go into Phase Three: Start without that committee established or without those criteria signed off, you're heading into a very high-risk environment. You'll always be that little bit behind and reacting to events. You might be thinking, "It's not that risky, we'll just let all of this happen in the background and we'll be fine." Are you sure about that? Setting yourself up for a project meltdown is not usually about one particular thing. It's about a series of small, almost invisible things across each of the Activity Domains that keep adding up, until the unravelling is clearly apparent and can no longer be avoided.

Please make sure your governance systems, processes and structures are clearly developed *before* you start. Every organisation will have its own process for authorising arrangements, and this will come with fairly predictable timelines for achieving sign-off on a number of the elements you need for this Pre-Start phase. It will also give you a guide for how long this phase might take.

Another critical part of governance for Phase Two is to make sure service providers and contractors have a signed contract or agreement. This point is so obvious that you might be thinking it's hardly worth a mention. I agree, but it's frequently overlooked. Service providers or contractors start in good faith, without a contract, because they are well known and/or because of time pressure to start. In my experience, when this happens, I already know these critical stakeholders also haven't been fully briefed and don't clearly understand the project purpose, scope and objectives. If you talk to them individually, they'll all have a different impression of the goal. In other words, it's a key indicator of a team that is not skilled at managing a roll-out effectively and are not likely to achieve successful outcomes.

PROJECT / PROGRAM NAME:	
SUCCESS IS:	
	Phase Two: Pre-Start
Activity Domains	**Phase Goal:** Be operationally ready to begin service
Governance	Tie up loose ends from Phase One
	Authorise grants program criteria / tender specifications
	Confirm service provider contracts – for those starting on day one
	Establish working group
	Host first steering committee – ratify *Terms of Reference*
	Host first working group – ratify *Terms of Reference*
	Establish any other committee in your structure

Figure 2: Ghanvey Magnificent Matrix cut out. LifeCycle Phase Two: Pre-Start. Activity Domain – Governance

This Ghanvey Magnificent Matrix cut out is a sample of the sorts of tasks that might appear in the Governance Activity Domain, in Phase Two: Pre-Start. Your own project might look quite different.

Your turn.

ACTIVITY

In the cut out below from the Ghanvey Magnificent Matrix, dot point the tasks you need to complete in Governance, during Phase Two: Pre-Start.

Ghanvey LifeCycle Phase One Pre-Start *Pre-Start*

THE GHANVEY MAGNIFICENT MATRIX

PROJECT / PROGRAM NAME:	
SUCCESS IS:	
	Phase Two: Pre-Start
Activity Domains	**Phase Goal:** Be operationally ready to begin service
Governance	

Financial Management

In Phase One, the attention was on planning where the bigger chunks of money across each of the LifeCycle phases was needed. You did this to make sure you'll have enough money to get you through the duration of the project. Now, we're going to take one of those chunks and spend it.

To figure out what is needed in LifeCycle Phase Two: Pre-start, think about what starting actually looks like. What would make 'day one' work smoothly? Here are some questions as a guide.

- are you going to recruit new staff using a recruiting firm or are you doing that yourself?
- salaries – full-time, part-time, short-term, long-term? At what level?
- what equipment will those people need?

- what training do these people and existing people need?
- will you need some external support to help with strategy or maybe drafting specifications for a technical procurement that is coming up in the next LifeCycle Phase?
- will you have a pre-start stakeholder forum or training seminar to get everyone on the same page?
- are you outsourcing establishment of an evaluation framework?

By asking these few simple questions, it becomes clear where the money should be allocated. In case you didn't notice, those questions came from across the other Activity Domains. If you look at the actions happening across the Activity Domains, you'll know what to allocate for spending in LifeCycle Phase Two, or in any phase, for that matter.

In Phase Two, you'll be spending money on recruitment and training for all staff (including volunteers), purchasing everyday IT equipment and other equipment needs (e.g., phones, laptops and chairs). If you need a dedicated space, then include rent and fit-out. You get the idea. After all of these things go on your list, start to consider the not-so-everyday expenditures, like that 'one-off' source of external help, or the costs of conducting an introductory stakeholder forum. Maybe a vehicle is needed, as a pooled resource. Like I've said previously, working all this out is not rocket science, it just requires proactive, quick and dedicated thinking from that person who loves detailed planning. Hopefully this person and this sort of role will exist in your team. If not, you will need to figure out how to access those skills.

Ghanvey LifeCycle Phase One  Pre-Start

Figure 3 (below) contains lists of financial bits and pieces that might pop up in Phase Two. It's definitely not exhaustive, just a guide to prompt your thinking.

Figure 3: Phase Two resources to consider

An important part of this is the fact that there are probably existing policies and procedures for most of the things you need to do in this phase. There will be policies and/or procedures for recruitment, provisioning, purchasing equipment, establishing committees, IT systems... The most exciting thing about policies and procedures is that someone else has already thought through how it all works. That's the hardest part, and it's all done. All you have to do is remember to access these guides and follow them. Another huge benefit of these lovely little documents is a significant saving in time, as approvals will be a lot quicker when you're following authorised policies and procedures.

Don't be the clueless team who wastes precious dollars by not being prepared. You'll create delays and compromise outcomes even before the project has started. Is that what you really want?

When I was writing this chapter, I checked in with my own Office Manager, just to make sure I had covered all the details. Martine was phenomenal in raising so many of those fiddly tasks that I hadn't even thought about, and she encouraged me to break down the bigger tasks (like recruitment) into steps. Thank you, Martine, I know I would be lost without you!

Now let's include Financial Management in the Ghanvey Magnificent Matrix cut out so we can build a picture of the range of tasks that need to be completed during Phase Two.

Ghanvey LifeCycle Phase One   Pre-Start   *Pre-Start*

THE GHANVEY MAGNIFICENT MATRIX

PROJECT / PROGRAM NAME:	
SUCCESS IS:	
	Phase Two: Pre-Start
Activity Domains	**Phase Goal:** Be operationally ready to begin service
Governance	Tie up loose ends from Phase One
	Authorise grants program criteria / tender specifications
	Confirm service provider contracts – for those starting on day one
	Establish working group
	Host first steering committee – ratify *Terms of Reference*
	Host first working group – ratify *Terms of Reference*
	Establish any other committee in your structure
Financial Management	Tie up loose ends from Phase One
	Stakeholder forum
	Recruitment
	Salaries
	Equipment/provisioning
	Technical expertise
	Sessional Fees – expert advisory committee
	Confirm allocation of grants/service provider contracts/agreement payments

Figure 4: Ghanvey Magnificent Matrix cut out. LifeCycle Phase Two: Pre-Start. Activity Domains – Governance and Financial Management

This Ghanvey Magnificent Matrix cut out is a sample of the sorts of tasks that might appear in the Financial Management Activity Domain, in Phase Two: Pre-Start. Your own project might look quite different.

Rock your Roll Out

Your turn:

> ### ACTIVITY
> In the cut out below from the Ghanvey Magnificent Matrix, dot point the tasks you need to complete in Financial Management, during Phase Two: Pre-Start.

	Phase Two: Pre-Start
Activity Domains	**Phase Goal:** Be operationally ready to begin service
Governance	
Financial Management	

Stakeholder Engagement and Communication

The project team needs to be crystal clear when communicating with stakeholders about the project or program purpose, scope and objectives, and what their part is in that context. This means communicating furiously during the Pre-Start phase, to get everybody ready.

Ghanvey LifeCycle Phase One — Pre-Start

Please don't skip this bit! There is always something to learn, even if you're already pretty good with stakeholders. Remember, a curious mind always asks, "How does this apply to me?" "Why do I need a curious mind?" you might ask. "Because it keeps you alert to potential problems and opportunities and it is the best form of continuous improvement," would be my response. Curiosity transforms your role from a 'tick the list' job to a 'join the dots' responsibility that is focused on outcomes success. It still surprises me how often stakeholder engagement and communication are taken for granted. This ends up biting the project team later. Just because you might know your stakeholders well, that doesn't mean you can skip the bit where you need to communicate effectively with them.

Let me start with a caveat. I'm not a communications expert, so I'm not going to offer specialist tips on communication styles. My focus here is on the engagement and communication approach. Communicating effectively during Phase Two means tailoring your engagement appropriately to each category of stakeholders. This might be a formal letter to some groups and an informal newsletter to others, in a range of relevant languages. It might also include a forum for service providers where the project is explained in full and/or where they receive some introductory training. Appropriate communication might also consist of an infographic that provides a visual account of what is happening, or the offer of one-to-one support to make sure everyone is fully prepared to start on day one.

A couple of years ago, I got a call from a client who wanted me to 'translate' a set of guidelines from government language to community sector language. When the team manager telephoned, let's say her name is Elaine, I was baffled. Government guidelines come out all the time and they're usually pretty good. I thought this could be an easy job, so I accepted it. I was wrong. When I saw the 126-page set of guidelines for community workers, I couldn't believe it.

"How could anyone in their right mind believe that community workers have time to read this many pages?" I asked Elaine.

"That's why I called you," she said. "And wait till you read it. It's really dense."

She was right. This communication exercise had really missed the target. It was meant to guide community workers to understand reforms in their field and how this impacted on the way they did their jobs every day. However, instead of speaking to community workers, the document only spoke to government officials. The important pieces of information that community workers needed to know for their everyday practice were buried in patches throughout the document. It was truly the worst attempt at communication I had ever seen. The people who wrote it were really smart, but they didn't know who they were talking to. They were legal experts who had not had much involvement with community workers on the ground. Anyone who knew the sector would have known this audience had huge caseloads of vulnerable people to support, with few resources. In other words, they were overworked and stressed, with no time to spare for reading bulky documents.

Elaine and I worked together to make a 15-page document with relevant information in an easy format. In it, the changed practice piece they were trying to convey was much easier to find. The 'translated' guide was well-received by the community sector and formed part of their training package as they transitioned to the changed environment.

So, what's the moral of the story? Don't just send out 'one size fits all' material and think you've done your job.

That would be a 'tick the list' type of approach. It's not good enough and it won't return results. If you need stakeholders to be ready on day one of your 3P delivery, then view your role as a responsibility to join the dots and get the outcomes. Put yourself in the stakeholder's shoes and focus attention on their needs. If you have an opportunity to ask their representatives how they best receive information, take it. Use every avenue you can to be well-informed about your stakeholders so you can communicate with them in ways they will understand.

As with every step of this project management journey, I'm hoping you have access to these skills internally, preferably in your team. If not, you have the task of figuring out how to access them. Maybe try borrowing from another team, contracting in, or seeking advice from a trusted mentor or Critical Friend.

Many years ago, I saw a brilliant example of communicating to a particular stakeholder category. On this occasion, the category was Indigenous women in a specific age group. The government agency communicating a health message to them had thoughtfully outsourced development of the communication material to an Indigenous-owned and operated consultancy. The result was perfect and resonated with the target audience. What I saw was beautifully visual with key messages reduced to a single statement. It was also quite different to the standard material about the health message. The culturally-specific nature of the designed message meant those Indigenous women had access to a very important health message they could act on that might not have reached them through standard communication.

Thinking of your own 3P roll-out, build some stakeholder categories. Remember to allow for hidden stakeholders who may be passive. I have provided an example in Figure

5, below. The categories are only suggestions to guide you. There are lots of different ways to carve up categories and you'll know what is best for your own set of circumstances.

Activity: Stakeholder Categories.

1. *Identify relevant stakeholder themes for your 3P roll-out.*
2. *Under the themes, identify stakeholder categories.*
3. *Dot point the individuals, committees and organisations who will need to have a voice and/or be informed about your 3P roll-out.*
4. *Identify the engagement LifeCycle phase for each dot point.*
5. *Put yourself in the shoes of each dot point and see what they want to know and how they best receive information.*

DECISION-MAKERS AND ADVISORS	PROJECT SERVICES	WIDER INTEREST
Decision-makers	Operational	Other interested groups
Partners	Dependencies	Sector bodies
Collaborators	Interdependencies	Media

Figure 5: Identifying Stakeholder Categories for Engagement

Well done!

Now, let's take a look at how Stakeholder Engagement builds the Ghanvey Magnificent Matrix in Phase Two.

Ghanvey LifeCycle Phase One Pre-Start

THE GHANVEY MAGNIFICENT MATRIX

PROJECT / PROGRAM NAME:	
SUCCESS IS:	

Activity Domains	Phase Two: Pre-Start
	Phase Goal: Be operationally ready to begin service
Governance	Tie up loose ends from Phase One
	Authorise grants program criteria / tender specifications
	Confirm service provider contracts – for those starting on day one
	Establish working group
	Host first steering committee – ratify *Terms of Reference*
	Host first working group – ratify *Terms of Reference*
	Establish any other committee in your structure
Financial Management	Tie up loose ends from Phase One
	Stakeholder forum
	Recruitment
	Salaries
	Equipment/provisioning
	Technical expertise
	Sessional Fees – expert advisory committee
	Confirm allocation of grants/service provider contracts/agreement payments
Stakeholder Engagement	Tie up loose ends from Phase One
	Confirm Phase Two key message for stakeholder categories
	Design tailored communication for each stakeholder category
	Prepare stakeholders to play their part on day one – e.g., practice guidelines
	Stakeholder forum/training seminars

Figure 6: Ghanvey Magnificent Matrix cut out. LifeCycle Phase Two: Pre-Start. Activity Domains – Governance, Financial Management and Stakeholder Engagement.

The above table is a sample of the sorts of tasks that might appear in the Stakeholder Engagement and Communication Activity Domain, in Phase Two: Pre-Start. Your own project might look quite different.

Your turn:

> **ACTIVITY**
>
> In the cut out below from the Ghanvey Magnificent Matrix, dot point the tasks you need to complete in Stakeholder Engagement and Communication, during Phase Two: Pre-Start.

PROJECT / PROGRAM NAME:	
SUCCESS IS:	
	Phase Two: Pre-Start
Activity Domains	**Phase Goal:** Be operationally ready to begin service
Governance	
Financial Management	
Stakeholder Engagement	

Ghanvey LifeCycle Phase One   Pre-Start

Capability Management

To start with a quick refresh, capability is about having the right environment and skills to manage the 3P roll-out effectively across three tiers: a capable organisation; a capable team; a capable service provider. Looking back on the Post-Budget Planning phase, capability needs were planned across the entire project duration. Once again, begin this phase with a picture of what you need for a strong start to 3P delivery. You might start by looking for previous examples of 3P roll-outs by this organisation and read the evaluations of them. You might also talk to some of the team members who have managed previous 3P roll-outs, if they are still around. Learn what you can about the elements that worked well and the elements that didn't work so well in those cases.

While external specialty skills may be needed down the track, you are most likely going to need three key categories of internal skills in your team to start with: content expertise, administration expertise and social purpose project management expertise. Making sure these skills are on board and largely in-house from the start will be vital to moving the roll-out forward competently and confidently. The Pre-Start phase will be used for recruiting people with requisite skills and lifting capability through training. If you have a one-person 'team', your emphasis will need to be on lifting capability to fill any gaps and securing access to mentors.

"How can I be self-aware about my own gaps?" I hear your ask. You'll know if you're a content expert, so that one is a no-brainer. That doesn't mean you won't stop learning or refining your expertise, but it does mean you're able to run the content side of the project at hand.

By administrative expertise, I mean familiarity and confidence with the systems and processes in your organisation. How much lead time do you need for signoffs on different things? Can you confidently pay invoices and contracts? What's the timetable of annual events in the sector that impact your work, like Parliamentary Sitting Dates for government staff? If you're not particularly confident with these sorts of things, be proactive and learn them fast. Read documents and talk to people. Most 3P teams I've seen are relatively small, so everyone in the team should be an administrative expert (or adequately competent, at least), otherwise you're going to roll into slow motion without realising it.

Finally, by social purpose project management expertise, I mean understanding and applying a consistent method for the implementation of a dedicated project or program. It doesn't have to be the Ghanvey method (although I'd prefer if it is!), just a good and consistent method that means you build capability around consistency and achieve sustainable success.

Phase Two is about making sure these three layers of capability are in place before you transition to Phase Three and open the doors.

Think of service providers as part of your extended team. I have seen many cases where the service provider was well-known to the funder and there was an assumption that, just because they had done well in the past, they would be fine this time, too. This is not always the case. These people live in the real world too, and unpredictable stuff happens. Check in with service providers to make sure they can deliver for you. Probe under the surface to make sure you're satisfied that your 3P roll-out is in good hands.

Ghanvey LifeCycle Phase One   Pre-Start

Preparing and supporting service providers to be ready to deliver on your behalf — and to the standard you expect — is also an important part of this phase. You may need to help your service providers to help you. For example, you might include them in your training if it's relevant, or fund/subsidise their training. Remember, if your service providers struggle to meet targets, then you're struggling too.

Let's see how managing capability tasks adds to the Ghanvey Magnificent Matrix for Phase Two: Pre-Start.

Rock your Roll Out

THE GHANVEY MAGNIFICENT MATRIX

PROJECT / PROGRAM NAME:

SUCCESS IS:

Activity Domains	Phase Two: Pre-Start **Phase Goal:** Be operationally ready to begin service
Governance	Tie up loose ends from Phase One Authorise grants program criteria / tender specifications Confirm service provider contracts – for those starting on day one Establish working group Host first steering committee – ratify *Terms of Reference* Host first working group – ratify *Terms of Reference* Establish any other committee in your structure
Financial Management	Tie up loose ends from Phase One Stakeholder forum Recruitment Salaries Equipment/provisioning Technical expertise Sessional Fees – expert advisory committee Confirm allocation of grants/service provider contracts/agreement payments
Stakeholder Engagement	Tie up loose ends from Phase One Confirm Phase Two key message for stakeholder categories Design tailored communication for each stakeholder category Prepare stakeholders to play their part on day one – e.g., practice guidelines Stakeholder forum/training seminars
Capability Management	Tie up loose ends from Phase One Learn from previous 3P roll-outs in the organisation Prepare job descriptions for recruitment, specific to skills gaps Conduct recruitment process Onboard new staff – administration, systems and project induction Prepare job specs to bring in technical expert to write technical specifications for tender Source relevant training to lift internal capability Check in with service providers to make sure they are ready for day one Support service providers if needed

Figure 7: Ghanvey Magnificent Matrix cut out. LifeCycle Phase Two: Pre-Start. Activity Domains – Governance, Financial Management, Stakeholder Engagement and Capability Management.

Ghanvey LifeCycle Phase One Pre-Start

The Ghanvey Magnificent Matrix cut out above is a sample of the sorts of tasks that might appear in the Capability Management Activity Domain, in Phase Two: Pre-Start. Your own project might look quite different.

Your turn:

ACTIVITY

In the cut out below from the Ghanvey Magnificent Matrix, dot point the tasks you need to complete in Capability Management, during Phase Two: Pre-Start.

PROJECT / PROGRAM NAME:	
SUCCESS IS:	
	Phase Two: Pre-Start
Activity Domains	**Phase Goal:** Be operationally ready to begin service
Governance	
Financial Management	
Stakeholder Engagement	
Capability Management	

As you can see with examples from just four of the six Activity Domains, there is a lot to do in LifeCycle Phase Two: Pre-Start, and it's going to take dedicated attention to get it all done in a timely manner.

Transition to LifeCycle Phase Three

To transition to Phase Three, you need to have tied up any loose ends from Phase One and have at least 80 percent of Phase Two completed – not just underway but completed. You'll need to be honest about whether you are truly ready to 'open the doors'. That's why you'll call in your Critical Friends to help you assess whether you're ready.

There may be some of you thinking, "What a drag. I don't want Critical Friends holding me back." Let me assure you, they are not holding you back. They are saving you from yourself. Being challenged about the assumptions you're making as you prepare to open the doors could save you from steering off course. Bringing your attention to critical gaps that need closing can reduce risks of implosion in a later phase. This pool of people is going to be the best friends you ever have.

Conclusion

When I was developing the Ghanvey method, I toyed with a decision about whether to make LifeCycle Phase Two: Pre-start separate or join it to either the Post-Budget Planning phase or the Start phase. The deciding factor that prompted me to keep it as a separate phase was the tragic consequences of not completing these sorts of tasks before opening those proverbial (or indeed literal) doors on day one of service.

Ghanvey LifeCycle Phase One Pre-Start

Too many times, I witnessed lagging recruitment, governance on the run and smart content experts trying their best to cover all bases with limited additional skills and ultimately limited success. I've seen stakeholders who weren't briefed properly and headed off in the wrong direction from day one, unnoticed.

Given the significant experience in risk prevention I've had in my professional career, I often find myself thinking about better ways of doing things to prevent problems from happening in the first place. In my work, I realised that I simply couldn't let those negative consequences get a foothold in 3P roll-outs so early. For me, prevention was the sensible pathway for keeping those projects on the straight and narrow. I decided that focused attention was needed on those 1001 fiddly tasks from the outset to prevent problems from even starting. Phase Two had to stay, to give my beloved 3P roll-outs the best possible chance of achieving their desired outcomes.

Chapter 8: Key Messages

1. The 1001 fiddly tasks that prepare the 3P roll-out for day one are a legitimate and real part of doing.

2. Focused attention is needed to make sure the project is ready to 'open the doors' on day one.

3. Being ready to 'open the doors' means that everyone who plays a part on day one is briefed, capable and understands their role.

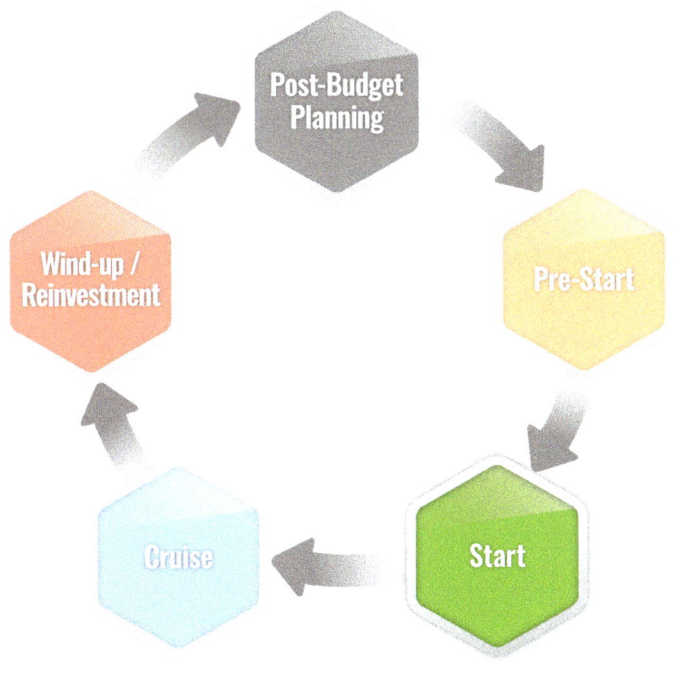

CHAPTER 9

Ghanvey LifeCycle Phase Three:
Start

Introduction

You've done your big picture planning in Phase One and you've completed 1001 fiddly and detailed operational readiness activities in Phase Two. This means you're ready to 'open the doors' on day one for your strategic program or project delivery. Day one can be exciting and daunting at the same time. If you've done your planning homework and communicated effectively with your stakeholders, then you should be confident the program will work. Nevertheless, we are human beings, so even with great planning there's probably going to be a few gaps here and there, just to keep you on your toes.

In this chapter, we're going to explore a quasi-'agile' approach for Phase Three. In this approach, you're assessing how everything is working once the doors are open and making refinements to reduce gaps and overcome blockers so the project can continue to move forward. Wondering what to assess? Zoom in on the Activity Domains. This is where reviewers and auditors always look to judge performance and it's for a very good reason. These Activity Domains are indicators of project health so checking in with them can expose previously hidden gaps.

In other words, this is the fail-fast phase. There are opportunities in this time to change your settings so you can make sure your Cruise phase is comfortable by the time you get there. By comfortable, I don't mean it will be easy, or that you'll be relaxing with your feet up and sipping a cocktail. By a comfortable Cruise phase, I mean one that is low-risk and outcomes-focused for the funder and the clients. If you learn to **find problems early and fix them fast** during LifeCycle Phase Three, your 3P roll-out will retain momentum and be far more likely to stay on track. Early detection means that the 'fails' will be small and relatively easy to fix, minimising disruption to project progress.

If you ignore this phase and fail slowly along the way, your 'fail' will likely have grown in size and dimension and be a big bombshell waiting to explode by the time you're prepared to do anything about it. It's hit high-level, red-flag risk status, by then. Despite the imminent risk, it's going to be much more difficult and time-consuming to fix, because

Ghanvey LifeCycle Phase One   Start

whatever it is, it's already embedded. We all know how hard it is to bring change to the familiar. What's more, if this thing — a clunky governance structure, for example — is not working, then it has already been damaging the project for an extended period of time. That means you've probably sucked the life blood out of your project already, making it more challenging to turn around. You get the picture.

Let's take a look at how to do Phase Three: Start really well so you have the best possible chance of seeing through a 3P roll-out successfully. In this chapter, I'll pull out the Activity Domains of governance, financial management and capability management.

Day One and Beyond

Phase Three: Start is all about opening the doors on day one and letting the clients in, so to speak. It might be about running a grants program, a reform program, or beginning some new strategic initiatives. Regardless of your own scenario, you're starting the delivery and you're going to test if you have all the settings right across the Activity Domains. If you've done your homework well across LifeCycle Phases One and Two, these items should be crystal clear, and everyone will be on the same page to start.

If you didn't have time to set a strong foundation and just had to start, then actions against Activity Domains are likely to be mushy, i.e., not crystal clear, so you're not able to test anything. "What's the difference between mushy and clear?" I hear you ask. If you really want to know the details, you can go back to Chapter 4 and do an activity to practice. For now, a broad illustration is for me to ask you, "What do you want to achieve with your 3P roll-out?" A mushy answer is "world peace." A clear answer to that question is SMART:

Specific, Measurable, Achievable, Relevant and Time-bound. It would be along the lines of: "To develop a statewide, real-time, secure safe-house register for family violence victim support services to access by June 2025."

A mushy roll-out will simply unfold 'organically' (code word for 'chaotically' if ever I heard one) and you'll react to whatever comes up. About six to eight months in, you'll probably need to retrofit clarifying elements from Phase One and Two, because you've lost so much control. The reason you can't test anything when you start with a mushy objective is that it's too broad to be effectively measured. It's more of a concept than a pragmatic project.

Put yourself in the shoes of a project service provider who is tasked with the action part of this project. Which one do you think would be successful? The 'World Peace' project or the 'Safe-house Register' project? Inexperienced collaborators might think "World peace, yeah, we want that, too," and get a bit excited, but they'll soon figure out they don't know where the destination is or when they're supposed to arrive. They will also soon realise they're not quite sure what actions they're supposed to commit to in order to help. On the other hand, the 'Safe-house Register' project is clearly defined. Instantly, you are confident about what the project is aiming to achieve. You can picture the outcome or destination and you know when you're supposed to arrive. That means you can plan your resources to make it happen.

Remember the Sat Nav metaphor? It's quite a handy picture here. If you only have mushy instructions, the Sat Nav won't even take you off the start line. You'll just sit there, stationary. If you enter clear instructions, the Sat Nav will take you to your destination via the shortest possible route

Ghanvey LifeCycle Phase One   **Start**

and also save you a lot of time by avoiding traffic blockers along the way.

Even with the best laid plans, there will be problems, both big and small, that will only be known after starting. This is normal and there is no need to yell at anyone when it happens. Be realistic, expect problems to arise and be prepared to respond to them. Make sure there is at least one experienced team member whose workload is designed to be flexible during those first few weeks or months, enabling them to respond to problems quickly if they need to.

Setting a Timeframe for Phase Three

For those who are ready to start confidently or who are willing to retrofit, it's really important to set a meaningful period of time in which you seek useful feedback about your 3P delivery settings. Feedback can come in many different ways. It could be from testing the way decisions are made, observing how processes are working, or finding out the way service design is impacting users. A meaningful timeframe to get this sort of feedback might be three to four weeks for a one-year, straightforward roll-out, or six months or more for a large, complex roll-out.

How will you know what timeframe is the best fit for your particular 3P roll-out? It depends on the nature and scope of the project, and what's going on across the six Activity Domains. Let me illustrate this through an example of decision-making. To really test if the project governance structure is working, your Phase Three needs to allow enough time for a range of decisions to be made. For example:

- small everyday decisions that are made by the team manager or leader, such as authorising provisioning for a new staff member

- medium-sized decisions that need an extra level of signoff above the team manager (probably from an executive), such as hiring a consultant who needs to be paid more than the manager is allowed to approve
- significant, strategic decisions about the project that need to go to a higher-level executive or steering committee attached to the project. This might be something like authorising the whole-of-project phased implementation plan, or approving a tender

Team size won't necessarily be the gauge here. A team of one running a straightforward project might be able to identify the blockers that are slowing down decision-making within three weeks, because their systems are relatively streamlined. On the contrary, a team of four may take a couple of months to figure out where the decision-making blockers are coming from, because they are likely to be working on a much larger, more complex project roll-out where decision-making is more diffused. This team may have to wait for several committee meetings to pass before a pattern emerges.

When a 3P roll-out has a steering committee that has to authorise the big decisions — be they strategic guidance or large dollar value commitments — there is probably a regular timeframe that this body meets. If it's once a month, you'll have a better chance of assessing its merits quickly. If it meets every second month or each quarter, you may only choose to include one or two meetings in the Phase Three period. This might not be enough meetings to really understand whether problems exist and whether they'll slow down the project. It might be a case of making the transition to Phase Four: Cruise (when you will be actively managing and monitoring the roll-out) with an agreement in place for

Ghanvey LifeCycle Phase One   Start

a 12-month structured program of ongoing assessment and revision.

There is no point setting a Phase Three timeframe of two weeks just because you're in a hurry and want to get this stuff out of the way as soon as possible. Remember, you're already delivering the program or project at this stage, so even the dedicated doers among you can't complain that this is getting in the way of 'doing' implementation. This is doing, efficiently.

This close attention to how the project is working once the doors have opened will help you reduce your risks and increase your chance of success. Ultimately, it will save you a lot of time and resources, because when a project is working well, stakeholders can see it and feel it. When they can see it and feel it, they tend to stay with you and redouble their efforts to help you succeed. When a project is stalling and constantly making excuses for being stuck in the mud, stakeholders can see and feel that, too, and they tend to drop their level of interest and support proportionally.

Working the Activity Domains in Phase Three

	Phase Three: Start
Activity Domains	Phase Goal: Begin 3P service, identify problems and fix them fast
Governance	
Financial Management	
Stakeholder Engagement	
Capability Management	
Risk Management	
Outcomes & Benefits Management	

PROJECT / PROGRAM NAME:
SUCCESS IS:

Figure 1: Ghanvey Magnificent Matrix cut out. LifeCycle Phase Three: Start

There is no time for being polite and making excuses during this phase. I hasten to add, that doesn't mean we let the cowboys in. It's always time for respect and inclusion. The focus here is on what is *not* serving the drive towards the 3P roll-out goal. If you're not sure, start listening to what you're complaining about and check in about what's making you feel frustrated. Your answers will be the blockers and they must shift.

It's extraordinary how many times blockers are well known but remain in place because it's 'too hard' to change them. The catch cry of Phase Three is: **"Find problems early and fix them fast."** Resolving blockers is a critical part of actively managing implementation. Choose to be proactive and professional.

"How will I know if the Activity Domains are working as they should?" I hear you ask. Good question. To know what is and is not serving your 3P roll-out, you have to know what success looks like. If we go back to our 'Safe-house Register' project example from earlier, the objective gives us a clear picture of success: the development of a statewide, real-time, secure safe-house register, accessible in real time to services that need to place victims of family violence in this housing. We also know that it needs to be ready by June 2025. Once you have an equivalent clear picture for your project, ask yourself, *"What would it take to go from what we have now, to that picture, in that timeframe?"* The answer to that question effectively reveals the actions to apply to the six Activity Domains.

Let's run a simple test across a few Activity Domains so you can get the idea. Using the 'Safe-house Register' project as our example, we'll ask, "What would it take to go from what we have now, to that picture, in that timeframe?" Let's say the current context is that there is no common register. Services currently work together by calling around with each other when they need to place a client. This leaves us with a lot to do, and we'll assume we have a budget, and the timeframe is quite tight.

The test is based on three simple questions:

- what do we need?
- is that happening?
- if not, where is the problem?

For this project, we're going to need a new IT system that services can access in real time, to place clients in need. That IT system does not currently exist. The key problem is that there are more than 50 different types of IT systems used across the sector, many of which are effectively obsolete. So, we're going to need to develop a set of technical specifications to develop the new IT system.

Governance

I realise I illustrated some governance issues in previous chapters, and you might be wondering why I have started with governance again, instead a different Activity Domain. Here's why. Governance is a massively significant part of 3P delivery success and is commonly poorly understood and executed. In my experience, it's often the source of so many problems that masquerade as different, myriad smaller problems in other Activity Domains. Timeline blowout is a classic example of this and is often caused by slow decision-making, which is caused by a clunky governance structure with too many layers.

So, here we go.

Question 1: What would it take in our 3P governance to go from what we have now to an active register by June 2025, when there's a lot to do? Answer: informed and quick decisions.

Ghanvey LifeCycle Phase One   Start

Question 2: Is informed and quick decision-making happening? There's no easy answer here, you'll need to do some investigating.

We've had two steering committee meetings and they have given us all the decisions we asked for, but something isn't right. Staff are mostly on board, but there's one person who seems to be taking forever to join us and there's not enough computers to go around.

Don't assume that it's only committees and big decisions that slow things down. It's surprising sometimes how fast a massive decision can be made, while small items seem to take eons of time to work their way through the various systems. This means you'll need to observe and assess decision-making at all levels. Any blocker that slows progress is a problem and can throw the entire project off course.

Question 3: Where is the problem?

The blocker ends up being the in-tray of Executive X, who has been sitting on a recruitment signoff for several weeks, so you'll need to have a conversation with them. Find a respectful and firm way of illustrating to Executive X the impact of their in-tray delay and the risk it's causing to the entire 3P roll-out. Ask them what they need from you to support a faster turnaround. Being uncomfortable isn't a part of the equation, here. You'll just have to get past that. The conversation is not about you, it's about the project, so get yourself out of the way and work it out. You have an entire project relying on having that recruitment signed off. There are terrified victims of family violence relying on you to move that document through the system. Choose to persist.

If you're uncomfortable approaching a difficult conversation, search the internet for a 'how-to' lesson. Take someone with you if that helps, but have the conversation you must. In my experience, the problem is generally not a conspiracy against you personally, or against the project. That signoff might be stalling because Executive X prefers to talk it through first. It's simply the way they work, and you might not have noticed it before now. When you find this out, you'll know to always book a meeting before putting any documents in their in-tray.

The example I have given here assumes an exemplary steering committee, which is not always the case. If you find your steering committee has members who either don't turn up, regularly delegate to someone who is not authorised to make a decision or turn up unprepared because they're too busy to read the material, then you have a serious red flag for action. This sort of committee (which I have seen countless times), will only ever take you on the road to nowhere.

If your steering committee is troublesome, it may call for another difficult conversation with your executive and/or chair to prompt the reigning in of members. On the plus side, you're going to get really good at having difficult conversations by the time this 3P roll-out is over, which is a great skill to have. Once again, the focus of the conversation is going to be about the negative impact of the problem on the entire 3P roll-out, including the escalating risk of timeline and cost blowouts that this problem is causing. Emphasise the risks of not fixing it fast.

Here is a range of things you can test and check for Governance in Phase Three.

Ghanvey LifeCycle Phase One   Start   Start

THE GHANVEY MAGNIFICENT MATRIX

PROJECT / PROGRAM NAME:
SUCCESS IS:

	Phase Three: Start
Activity Domains	**Phase Goal:** Begin 3P service, identify problems and fix them fast
Governance	**Operational Actions** Tie up loose ends from Phase Two Host steering committee x 3 Host working group x 3 **Testing Actions** Are decisions being made quickly? Is the 3P governance structure effective? Are the key roles allocated to the right people? Are the committees working well? Are there too many? Are committee *Terms of Reference* hitting the mark? Are they all ratified? Are the key documents updated? Are we confident that the actions will achieve the outcome? Do we have Critical Friends lined up for our transition assessment?

Figure 2: Ghanvey Magnificent Matrix cut out. LifeCycle Phase Three: Start. Activity Domain – Governance

This Ghanvey Magnificent Matrix cut out is a sample of the sorts of tasks that might appear in the Governance Activity Domain, in Phase Three: Start. Your own project might look quite different.

Your turn:

ACTIVITY

In the cut out below from the Ghanvey Magnificent Matrix, dot point the tasks you need to complete in Governance, during Phase Three: Start.

THE GHANVEY MAGNIFICENT MATRIX

PROJECT / PROGRAM NAME:	
SUCCESS IS:	
	Phase Three: Start
Activity Domains	**Phase Goal: Begin 3P service, identify problems and fix them fast**
Governance	

Financial Management

Moving onto financial management now, remember that Phase One was about planning the budget allocation across each of the LifeCycle phases to align with the level of activity in the project at the time. In Phase Two, we started to spend some money on a range of relatively small project consumables. In Phase Three, we'll be starting to spend a bit more.

Question 1: What would it take in our 3P financial management to go from what we have now to an active register by June 2025, when there's a lot to do? Answer: to be able to spend the allocated funds on time.

Question 2: Are we spending the allocated funds on time? Time to do some quick investigating.

Ghanvey LifeCycle Phase One — Start

Sometimes the best way to figure out where the gaps are in financial management is to think about the annoying and frustrating financial things that you experience on the ground. Are they big, small, or both? Maybe it's those expert advisory members who always complain about not receiving their sessional fees. It might actually be true and need fixing. "Oh no, why don't I have access to that software program today? Does anyone else have the same problem?" Maybe that fabulous software where you entered all the details for the technical specifications that need to go out next week has vanished. And finally, a classic, "Oh wow, we've come in way under budget this month, what happened?"

Question 3: Where is the problem?

Those sessional fees forms might be sitting in a pile on somebody's desk, or maybe the processing system doesn't recognise that new code, so they're stuck in the system.

It might be a backlog of smaller invoices that haven't been paid, causing those services to cease – there goes that software package. Is the problem caused by an inexperienced person at the front end, a system with far too many steps, or a bottleneck at the end of the process where all the invoices from across the organisation come together? You'll have to find the weak link and fix it, fast.

If a service provider didn't meet targets, that means they didn't get paid. That's why you're way under budget this month. Not spending money that is committed is considered bad financial management, in fact, it's very bad financial management. There are lots of reviews and audits to back me up on that one.

Problems don't usually fix themselves and often become worse over time if they're left unchecked. They need conscious action to resolve. If you don't find them and fix them fast, they will individually and collectively drag the project down as it progresses.

Find the problems early and fix them fast, before they become the bugbear of your life and your failures become the legacy for which you gain notoriety. If the project was costed effectively, then you need that money to achieve the outcome. If you end up with a bucket of unspent funds, then what do you think the chances are of family violence victims benefiting from the safe-house service that's available from June 2025? It's not going to happen. How are those services going to keep that woman and her children safe without the register? Always remember the purpose of your project. This gives you the reason why you need to **find problems early and fix them fast**.

This is what the Ghanvey Magnificent Matrix for Phase Three: Start looks like with both Governance and Financial Management actions filled in.

Ghanvey LifeCycle Phase One   Start   *Start*

THE GHANVEY MAGNIFICENT MATRIX

PROJECT / PROGRAM NAME:	
SUCCESS IS:	
	Phase Three: Start
Activity Domains	**Phase Goal: Begin 3P service, identify problems and fix them fast**
Governance	**Operational Actions** Tie up loose ends from Phase Two Host steering committee x 3 Host working group x 3 **Testing Actions** Are decisions being made quickly? Is the 3P governance structure effective? Are the key roles allocated to the right people? Are the committees working well? Are there too many? Are committee *Terms of Reference* hitting the mark? Are they all ratified? Are the key documents updated? Are we confident that the actions will achieve the outcome? Do we have Critical Friends lined up for our transition assessment?
Financial Management	**Operational Actions** Tie up loose ends from Phase Two Contracts/Agreements payments Salaries Project consumables **Testing Actions** Is the budget tracking as anticipated? Are service providers being paid? Are the financial processes working well? Are the financial approvals working well? Have we had any financial surprises?

Figure 3: Ghanvey Magnificent Matrix cut out. LifeCycle Phase Three: Start. Activity Domains – Governance and Financial Management

This Ghanvey Magnificent Matrix cut out is a sample of the sorts of tasks that might appear in the Financial Management Activity Domain, in Phase Three: Start. Your own project might look quite different.

Your turn:

> **ACTIVITY**
>
> In the cut out below from the Ghanvey Magnificent Matrix, dot point the tasks you need to complete in Financial Management, during Phase Three: Start.

PROJECT / PROGRAM NAME:	
SUCCESS IS:	
	Phase Three: Start
Activity Domains	**Phase Goal: Begin 3P service, identify problems and fix them fast**
Governance	
Financial Management	

Capability Management

Now, let's look at capability management for Phase Three. Remember, in Phase One you would have planned the skills you needed across each of the LifeCycle phases and been clear about how to access these skills. You would have also mapped out how the organisation would learn from this project. In Phase Two, you would have started recruiting or contracting. In Phase Three, you'll be starting to test the skills on the ground, both internally and with service providers, if you have them.

Ghanvey LifeCycle Phase One — Start

Back to our safe house register project scenario.

Question 1: What would it take in our 3P capability management to go from what we have now to an active register by June 2025? Answer: skills and experience in social purpose project management, as well as content and specialist expertise on the ground when we need them.

Question 2: Do we have these skills on the ground to keep the 3P roll-out moving forward?

Note here that the answer is about skills and experience, not one or the other. It is critically important to have this combination in the people in key roles, at least. Content expertise is relatively easy to assess. Experience is more than just years in the workforce. It means a solid track record of successfully managing similar projects in the social purpose sector.

If you're lucky enough to have a team, it is likely to include a team member who has expertise but still needs experience with managing projects. Any team member who is not confident with social purpose project management overall or who has some 'blind spots' that need addressing will drag the project down. Capability gaps are important to find early and fix fast. A subscription to the Ghanvey library is always a good place to start if you want to build specific skills in social purpose project management or select a pool of Critical Friends for support throughout the project journey. **3pda.com.au/ghanvey/**

Back to our scenario. You did your capability planning in LifeCycle Phase One: Post-Budget Planning and recruited people with the skills you needed during Phase Two: Pre-start. Now you have all the requisite skills you need on the ground, but when you look closely, one of the senior project officers was meant to finalise that evaluation framework last week and you still don't have it. The other officer was supposed to host a working group this week, but it's been deferred for two weeks. That means we won't be able to offer an opinion to the steering committee next week, so a decision on the parameters for the register will have to wait until the following steering committee meeting, five weeks away.

Question 3: Where is the problem?

There are a few areas you can check to see if they reveal where the gaps are hiding. Are the skills applied to the 3P roll-out dedicated, or are they applied to this project on the side? By 'on the side' I mean in staff borrowed from different teams, or staff in the core team who have so many other responsibilities that they can hardly be counted as a resource. Are they available when you need them? Or, is it mostly a case of, "I can't come now, I'm up to my neck in briefings. How about next week?" If the project is stalling because you can't access the skills and experience you need when you need them, then it's not working. This is a common problem and is often let go as normal or possibly too awkward to address. Don't bury your head in the sand, **find the problem early and fix it fast**.

You might have to face another difficult conversation with an executive about the reality of skills on the ground and the negative impact this is having on the entire 3P roll-out. Remember to always have a solution ready when you have these conversations. Executives, chairs and other senior staff are very busy, and if you only take complaints to them, they might get the impression you're a whinger. If you offer solutions as well, they'll see you as a proactive leader.

Just for the record, the solution should not be to automatically outsource that piece of work the rarely available person hasn't done yet. That's not sustainable and will not build the internal capability that's vital to the organisation. You'll need to consider the appropriate balance between allocating key pieces of work to internal staff and external consultants. Remember to call your Critical Friends. They will be able to help you sort out the mess and get you back on track.

A few questions remain for the organisation, rather than the team.

Does the organisation have a development and training plan on social purpose project management to support effective and efficient implementation? If it does, make sure that everyone internally working on social purpose projects of any kind knows about it and uses it. If it doesn't, pull one together and advocate like mad to get it over the line. Managing social purpose projects is a professional skill and should be a standard competency for all internal staff involved in strategic programs, new initiatives, reform programs and innovation projects. If you enhance skills early and continuously, you'll reduce the risk of mistakes and increase the chance of achieving the outcomes you desire, because **consistency is the key to success**. This will also mean that the appropriate skills will always be available on the ground when they are needed.

When it comes to service providers, Phase Three is about checking that they're coping well. Does the service design need tweaking? Does the design of reporting need tweaking? Do their skills on the ground need tweaking? Remember, if they struggle, you struggle, so help them to help you. You should know the drill by now. Your role for Phase Three is to **find problems early and fix them fast**, otherwise you're just not going to be able to deliver the outcome.

Let's have a look at how Phase Three: Start is building in the Ghanvey Magnificent Matrix. It's beginning to show a busy picture of testing and revising.

Rock your Roll Out

PROJECT / PROGRAM NAME:	
SUCCESS IS:	

	Phase Three: Start
Activity Domains	**Phase Goal:** Begin 3P service, identify problems and fix them fast
Governance	**Operational Actions** Tie up loose ends from Phase Two Host Steering Committee x 3 Host Working Group x 3 **Testing Actions** Are decisions being made quickly? Is the 3P governance structure effective? Are the key roles allocated to the right people? Are the Committees working well? Are there too many? Are Committee *Terms of Reference* hitting the mark? Are they all ratified? Are the key documents updated? Are we confident that the actions will achieve the outcome? Do we have Critical Friends lined up for our transition assessment?
Financial Management	**Operational Actions** Tie up loose ends from Phase Two Contracts/Agreements payments Salaries Project Consumables **Testing Actions** Is the budget tracking as anticipated? Are service providers being paid? Are the financial processes working well? Are the financial approvals working well? Have we had any financial surprises?
Stakeholder Engagement	
Capability Management	**Operational Actions** Tie up loose ends from Phase Two Access to training for staff, volunteers and service providers Draft specifications for specialist expertise required in Phase Four **Testing Actions** Are the skills needed applied to the 3P roll-out in a timely manner? Did we get the Capability Plan right? Is the training program hitting the mark? Are there skills gaps we need to fill now? Can we see newly identified expertise that we'll need in Phase Four?
Risk Management	
Outcomes & Benefits Management	

Figure 4: Ghanvey Magnificent Matrix cut out. LifeCycle Phase Three: Start. Activity Domains – Governance, Financial Management and Capability Management

Ghanvey LifeCycle Phase One Start

This Ghanvey Magnificent Matrix cut out is a sample of the sorts of tasks that might appear in the Capability Management Activity Domain, in Phase Three: Start. Your own project might look quite different.

Your turn:

ACTIVITY

In the cut out below from the Ghanvey Magnificent Matrix, dot point the tasks you need to complete in Capability Management, during Phase Three: Start.

THE GHANVEY MAGNIFICENT MATRIX

PROJECT / PROGRAM NAME:	
SUCCESS IS:	
	Phase Three: Start
Activity Domains	**Phase Goal: Begin 3P service, identify problems and fix them fast**
Governance	
Financial Management	
Stakeholder Engagement	
Capability Management	
Risk Management	
Outcomes & Benefits Management	

As you can probably gather from taking this journey with me across the selected Activity Domains of governance, financial management and capability management, this phase is intense and needs dedicated attention. "There's no way we would do any of that, we would never have the time," I just heard someone say behind my back. My response to you is to remember that old adage, 'If you fail to plan, you plan to fail.' This is about lifting the social purpose profession. If you happened to change seats and your new seat was in the middle of an infrastructure project, you'd be doing all this and more because there would be a focus on delivering that tangible thing safely, securely, on time and within allocated resources. Is it really too much to expect the same from social purpose professionals whose projects serve the most vulnerable people in our community? I don't think so. The shift is already happening, so it will eventually catch up with you. Choose to be proactive and professional and take a leading role.

Remember, if you're in social purpose, you're mission driven. Even if your 3P roll-out is a strategic change, like an organisational merger, vulnerable clients are relying on you to get this right. Holding onto elements that are not working (because you might lose face if you admit they don't work) doesn't serve you, the organisation, or the client. Most of all, it doesn't serve the 3P roll-out, because those elements will undermine all the efforts that have been made to achieve the desired outcomes. It won't matter how many weekends you put in; it simply won't turn things around. Extra time will just continue to embed existing problems, which in turn, will continue to cause damage as you roll along.

No faith is lost when you put Phase Three 'on the table', because its whole purpose is to acknowledge human frailty, fail fast and fix fast. It's not about pointing the finger at individuals; it's about pointing the finger at the project.

Ghanvey LifeCycle Phase One   Start

LifeCycle Phase Three is all about how we make this 3P roll-out rock. When the roll-out is rocking, you'll be serving the social purpose profession, the organisation, the project and those vulnerable clients so much better.

Transition to LifeCycle Phase Four

Towards the end of LifeCycle Phase Three: Start, you'll need to decide if you're ready to transition to LifeCycle Phase Four: Cruise, or if you need extra time to reset a few things and test again. The decision to retest a few elements is not about the need to start – you've already done that. It's about keeping the 3P roll-out moving forward to achieve the outcome on time, with minimal risk and within allocated resources.

The aim for transition from LifeCycle Phase Three to Phase Four is not to be perfect, that's unrealistic. What is realistic is achieving a relatively smooth operation where the elements that need to work well are working well. It's about achieving a proactive and confident state, rather than a reactive and confused state.

Your Critical Friends should be called in to assess your progress and readiness to transition to LifeCycle Phase Four: Cruise. Don't even think about trying to do this yourself. The project team should prepare the material for the Critical Friends and then hand it over. It's always a bit frightening to do that, because you never know what someone else will say, but Critical Friends are your trusted companions. They know their role is to support you to get the best out of the project and help you move forward successfully. They want your 3P roll-out to rock.

Conclusion

It's extraordinary how many 3P roll-outs stay with structures, systems and significant skills gaps that are letting them down at every turn. No one 'owns' checking, tweaking and testing again. Rather than incorporate this function as a standard part of the way projects are approached, everyone simply buries their individual and collective heads in the sand and tries to struggle forward. You're human, right? Expect problems and give yourself permission to fail, as long as you fix it fast!

A consistent theme that runs through the range of formal reviews of disastrous social purpose program roll-outs is that it's never a single thing that causes the failure. It's a series of things: the steering committee didn't realise it was the key decision-maker; the coordinating team had low skills in project management; the service providers didn't have a clear brief... The confluence of these problems that no one checked then resulted in catastrophic failure. Lives were lost, heads rolled among the relevant leadership and vulnerable clients didn't end up with the services they needed.

Delivering the outcome is critical for the organisation and its clients and clearly a priority for your funder. That's why it's so important to separate these tasks into a dedicated phase. You need to practice the discipline of focusing attention on finding problems early and fixing them fast. If you go about this exercise in an organised way, by testing against the Activity Domains, you can get across it relatively calmly and quickly. It becomes a standard part of actively managing the implementation of the project.

If you don't deliberately look for emerging problems that are blocking ultimate success, you simply won't deliver your outcomes, and you could end up causing harm. Most

Ghanvey LifeCycle Phase One   Start

social purpose projects I've worked on and supported are funded because of dire need, not because they are nice to have. This means we have to find a system for achieving consistent success. Imagine if all the social purpose projects in the world achieved their goals! What a huge difference that would make. You are part of that difference and every choice you make to keep persisting actively contributes to positive social change.

Chapter 9: Key Messages

1. Find problems early and fix them fast.
2. Point the finger at the project, not at individuals.
3. Learn to have difficult conversations - get yourself out of the way – it's not about you, it's about the project.
4. Consistency is the key to success.

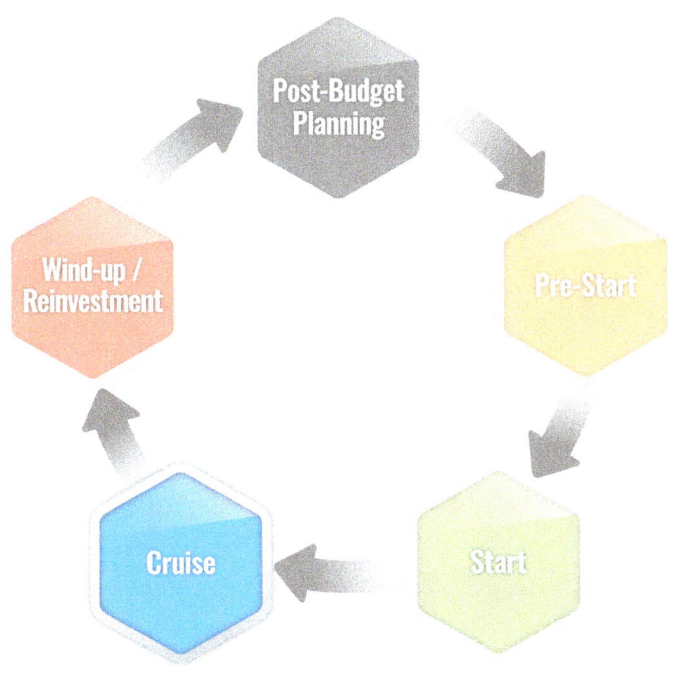

CHAPTER 10

Ghanvey LifeCycle Phase Four:
Cruise

Introduction

Now that you've set everything up well and tested and revised it, you reach LifeCycle Phase Four: Cruise. The Cruise phase is when the activities that will get you to your destination are rolling fairly smoothly. This phase is not as intense as the previous three, but it still needs focused attention. It's about **actively managing, monitoring, supporting and reporting**.

Just because things are working well, that's no reason to take your eyes off the ball. It is not the time to reallocate staffing resources to a long list of other things. 3P roll-outs need constant attention. Complacency will bring undone all the hard work with lightening speed. This phase is the highest risk phase for that very reason. You don't want to end up being named and shamed on a front-page media story about how you dropped the ball, so stay awake and pay attention.

You're going to be relying on a lot of human beings for your success during the Cruise phase and that means mistakes *will* be made. Expect them and keep your eyes and ears open for them. Learn from them. The vast majority of mistakes are not malicious conspiracies, they're just mistakes. Jumping all over the mistake-maker and setting their pants on fire is not going to serve your 3P roll-out.

Believe me, there is much to do across the Activity Domains that will help you to maintain continuous momentum, keep a lid on risk and make sure the activities being undertaken are the right ones to get you to that picture of success. The sorts of things you'll need to be doing during Phase Four: Cruise are:

- checking that governance remains lean and facilitates decision-making
- constantly assessing resource allocation to keep the budget on track
- maintaining stakeholder relationships
- maintaining capability as staff come and go
- assessing risks, especially in the wider environment
- collecting and analysing data and impact evidence
- deciding whether to wind-up or reinvest

Ghanvey LifeCycle Phase One   Cruise   *Cruise*

In this chapter, we'll take a look at how to keep the Cruise phase working well when it's a deliberate, standalone phase. As I've mentioned, it's all about the Activity Domains. By now you'll be so used to referring to them, those checks and balances are going to get faster and faster but will still maintain integrity. Your Critical Friends will come with you to help you solve wicked problems and support you to deliver the best possible project.

Working the Activity Domains in Phase Four

PROJECT / PROGRAM NAME:	
SUCCESS IS:	

Activity Domains	Phase Four: Cruise
	Phase Goal: Keep project stable and tracking to target
Governance	
Financial Management	
Stakeholder Engagement	
Capability Management	
Risk Management	
Outcomes & Benefits Management	

Figure 1: Ghanvey Magnificent Matrix cut out. LifeCycle Phase Four: Cruise.

Phase Four: Cruise is all about continuing to drive momentum towards the end goal. After all the intensity of Phases One through Three, it finally feels like you might have some breathing space. Yes, you can breathe a little easier, but don't fall asleep at the wheel, because you'll veer off course and potentially crash if you do.

Your Phase Four role is all about **managing, monitoring, supporting and reporting.**

Here's a simple overview of what I mean by those words in Box 1, below.

> **Managing** – continuing to coordinate the actions that will drive implementation towards the goal
>
> **Monitoring** – assessing Activity Domains to make sure relevant actions for all key bases are covered
>
> **Supporting** – if you rely on lagging service providers or staff with capability gaps, supporting them to lift performance
>
> **Reporting** – reporting progressive outcomes achievement against the specific KPIs and reporting project performance against the Activity Domains

Box 1: Overview of LifeCycle Phase Four role

Now let me tell you a story about why it's so important to perform this role really well during LifeCycle Phase Four: Cruise.

An innovation project I supported some years ago had veered off course and come within a hair's breadth of crashing because, once the project appeared to be set up and running, the senior leadership team just assumed all was well. Broadly speaking, it was a substance abuse project that was testing how to wrap other services around the vulnerable clients, while retaining the primary purpose of being a substance abuse program.

After setting up the project, the 'team of one' coordinator moved on and was duly replaced. The new incumbent had a strong background in mental health. The executive perceived this as a benefit because mental health is an important piece of those wraparound services. We all like to play to our strengths, and most of the time we do it unconsciously. That's exactly what happened here. The project started veering towards a focus on mental health. Mental health data started being collected and substance abuse stakeholders started to take a back seat, while new mental health related stakeholders were introduced to the table, and, well… you get the drift. After a period of several months, this innovation project turned into a mental health project.

When the hapless coordinator enthusiastically presented project progress to the organisation leadership team after 12 months, you can imagine how it went down. They were shocked and confused and more than a bit cross. "This innovation project was supposed to be about substance abuse and now we can't report on that. What are we going to tell the funder? This is going to make us look like a pack of dodos." The coordinator was equally confused and completely devastated.

There were a lot of problems to sort out for that project, starting with governance. The new project coordinator had arrived after the previous person left and the documentation wasn't very smart. That person had moved on with most of the information in their head. Next was a lesson for the executive about using the Activity Domains to check progress regularly, and to give their 'team of one' support through access to Critical Friends and other mentors.

I have told this tale because it's an example of a common problem and highlights the importance of paying attention across the entire duration of any 3P roll-out. Just for the record, the executive in this organisation had not properly understood how to approach the project and there were several holes in it by the time it got to a stage that essentially resembled Phase Four.

As with all the LifeCycle phases, the best health test is how well each of the Activity Domains is performing. If you check in with each Activity Domain regularly, you'll find problems early and be able to respond quickly. It's so easy to drop the ball when most things are in place and seem to be working well. Be warned, however – if you take a break during the Cruise phase, the outcomes will go on vacation, too.

During Phase Four, you'll also be collecting data against your agreed KPIs, so make sure you read what's coming in and start to understand the story it's telling.

"When do I check in with the Activity Domains?" I hear you ask. For the Cruise Phase, the answer is, "It depends." If your innovation project is 12 months long with a relatively limited Cruise duration, then a single Lifecycle transition check with Critical Friends would be sufficient. For a reform program of two years or more, there will be a transition assessment as you go into the Cruise phase, as well as regular mini health checks to make sure the 3P roll-out is continuing to drive momentum towards that goal.

A mini 'health check' is when Critical Friends support a quick assessment of progress against the Activity Domains to make sure everything is tracking as it should. I advise most clients with a longer-term project to do an initial health check at six months and again at 12 months. The reason I encourage a health check after six months is because I have seen so many projects begin to steer off course or show signs of serious break down at this time. In my experience, six to eight months into a project is the most critical time. Those with little to no consistency in their approach really start to fall apart at this point. Depending on what you find in these initial checks, you may want to continue with mini health checks every six months to make sure everyone is doing what they're supposed to. If you're confident you can stay the course, you can leave it to an annual health check, after the first 12 months.

If you're not up to where you should be in any given six-month period, it's a good idea to pull together a spontaneous mini health check with your Critical Friends, because you'll need to find the cause and fix it fast.

Let me be clear. Checking the health of a Cruise phase is not ticking off a checklist just for the sake of it. You and I both know that this would be a massive waste of time. The health check across the Activity Domains is to give you feedback about the relative health of your project, to identify gaps and provide the opportunity to respond to them quickly. It's keeping the mantra from Phase Three alive: **find problems early and fix them fast**. The health check is not an audit. It is future-focused, like the transition assessment. It looks at how likely you are to achieve your goals, given your current state of play. If you don't do these mini health assessments, you could very easily end up like our hapless coordinator, way off track.

In researching this book, I asked the many people I spoke to, "How are you managing to stay on top of your projects?" I was hoping to find some great examples of how to manage the Cruise phase well.

The common response was a deep breath followed by pursed lips and eyes looking up to the heavens, searching for words, until finally they were found. "We don't really do anything formal."

"Oh no," I could hear it coming. "If you tell me it's an organic process, I'll scream," I would say.

"It's an organic process..."

Let me say this loud and clear: There is no such thing as a coincidental, universal unfolding of a 3P roll-out that successfully delivers outcomes. Some parts may work quite well, but holistically it won't work well at all. Use a method. Of course, I recommend you use the Ghanvey method, but if you find another one that sits well with you, use that to stay on top of your roll-out and deliver consistently successful outcomes.

Before we drill down to look at some of the Activity Domains in a bit more detail, I just want to highlight a few more points about LifeCycle Phase Four.

The Wrinkles

It's important to acknowledge upfront that no project will ever be perfect, so we have to find ways of delivering the goal while living with a few project wrinkles along the way. That's entirely normal.

When wrinkles appear, it's the learning that is so important because that's what will take you towards your goal. For example, if someone inadvertently gives confidential papers to a service provider, please don't let your first response be to go and yell at them. That is a common response but it's a lose-lose situation. No one learns anything and the staff member is going to be too afraid to ask questions in future, which of course will lead to more mistakes. Be curious. Ask a few questions. Even better, discuss those questions. Here are some questions as a guide.

- how did that happen?
- was that person too afraid to ask a question or admit a lack of skills? If so, you need to fix your culture.
- is it the way our systems are set up that led people to make this mistake?
- is this an ongoing risk?
- what changes do we need to make to our systems to prevent this sort of mistake from happening again?

Okay, I think you get the drill. It's time to move onto some detail for a few of our Activity Domains so you can see what sort of actions you'll be taking during the Cruise phase.

Capability Management

As a quick reminder, capability management applies to the organisation, the team and service providers (if relevant).

Organisationally, the Cruise phase can easily end up being a time when leaders begin to cancel meetings, not show up to that steering committee, or delegate to someone who is not a decision-maker. "There's so much else to do and they're well on their way now. There's nothing to talk about. I don't have time for this anymore," they might say. Sound familiar? If that's what happens in your organisation, guess what happens to your 3P roll-out? That's right, it grinds to a halt. Without constant guidance, it can roll right off the end of the horizon. So many people who cancel meetings in this way don't join the dots about their role in a project's inevitable failure. Let me be clear about that right now. If that's you, then you have directly, albeit unintentionally, contributed to failure. When I say failure, I'm including the most common failure of all: partial success.

By partial success, I mean the 3P roll-out that has met some of the KPIs but not all of them. Consequently, the desired outcome is not met, and the benefits are not derived. There are lots of different reasons why projects fall short, many of which are legitimate. I have seen so many projects fall short for want of project management skills. For example, the project scope wasn't set properly, the objectives were not realistic or measurable, the governance overlay was strangling the project and/or there were big capability gaps, most often in financial management and risk management.

Evasive communication can dress up partial success as a win, but we all know it's not, except on *very* rare occasions. A classic case is reporting that, "250 participants successfully completed this program," while not revealing it was funded for 275 participants. We've all done it, and if you focus on project purpose, which should always be your guiding light, then it's a failure for the 25 people who missed out. This needs to be acknowledged, because it's through acknowledgement that we can find a solution. Here's part of the solution I prepared earlier: keep showing up at those meetings and ask questions about progress against the Activity Domains. There's a lot going on, all the way through the Cruise phase, so stay interested in the project purpose and outcome, and most of all, stay curious.

When it comes to capability in teams, the Cruise phase is high risk because people might come and go from the team for a hundred different reasons. Skills you were confident you had in your team the last time you checked are no longer there. Now the 3P roll-out team is slower and will potentially make more mistakes. The team may even be leading the charge in the wrong direction.

Ghanvey LifeCycle Phase One Cruise

One of the people who agreed to meet with me when I was researching for my Ghanvey digital learning platform revealed that his area had about ten projects on the go simultaneously, but only two people out of a dozen staff who had the skills to run them. He and the other executives were more than a little anxious that if one of those two got sick or left, they would be in a real dilemma.

"How can you live like that?" I asked.

"It's awful, but we just keep going."

I was incredulous. "Have you skilled up any of the other staff?"

"No, we're not sure what to do."

If ever there was a case of burying your head in the sand, this was it. These guys had managed to get to something that almost resembled the Cruise phase and then simply chosen to hope for the best, going forward. Is anyone with me if I call that just a tad irresponsible? "It's just life," I hear from a chorus of 3P professionals. Well, it doesn't have to be. Here's what you do.

During the Cruise phase, you can check in regularly to make sure the people with the skills you need are on the ground when you need them, so they contribute to driving implementation forward. If there are only two people out of 12 who have the requisite skills, then the primary thing you're contributing to is massive risk. You should urgently put a succession plan in place and have at least four to six more staff skilled up immediately, because when that many people are competent and confident, you'll be smashing out goals and mitigating risk at the same time.

It's also important to check in with those Critical Friends during the Cruise phase, because some of them may be able to mentor underdeveloped staff. Let them help you assess the skills you need, both presently and going forward.

Finally, choose a consistent approach or method for 3P roll-outs, to build competency and confidence right across the team. Remember our lesson? **Consistency is the key to success**. Of course, I recommend the Ghanvey method because it's been designed *by* a social purpose professional *for* social purpose professionals. At least there is now a clear option for learning dedicated social purpose project management skills. Nevertheless, as I stated earlier, if the Ghanvey method doesn't resonate with you, choose something else. Capability to drive the project towards success is a no-brainer, and having a consistent method is one of the easiest ways to lift capability.

The third dimension of capability is about service providers, if you are using them to help you meet outcomes. Service providers are real people too, who come and go from projects and who also need skills. If they struggle, you struggle. If they are supported to meet their targets, you meet your targets.

During the Cruise phase, you'll need to check in that your service providers still have the required skills on the ground. By checking in, I mean you should talk to them. A friend of mine who was 2IC at a large not-for-profit organisation received a letter from the government agency that provided some of their funding to inform them they had passed their program assessment. I can hardly do justice to the way she recounted her astonishment. "They didn't even talk to me. I had no idea we were being assessed. What is this secret assessment anyway?" So, what's the moral of the story? Pick up the phone. Even better – have a coffee, even if it's virtual. If your service provider has a big gap because the key case manager left and hasn't been replaced yet, it's likely to blow

Ghanvey LifeCycle Phase One   Cruise   *Cruise*

your entire project timeline. If you're **managing, monitoring, supporting and reporting** effectively, you'll find problems early. Just like Phase Three, your role is to fix those problems fast, because problems in one Activity Domain will impact others.

It's time to see how capability management looks in the Ghanvey Magnificent Matrix during LifeCycle Phase Four.

PROJECT / PROGRAM NAME:	
SUCCESS IS:	
	Phase Four: Cruise
Activity Domains	**Phase Goal: Keep project stable and tracking to target**
Governance	
Financial Management	
Stakeholder Engagement	

Capability Management	Tie up loose ends from Phase Three
	Regularly assess skills on the ground
	Update capability management plan annually
	    ■ Organisational capability
	    ■ Team capability (and succession skills plan)
	    ■ Service provider capability
	Provide access to skills uplift for all project staff
	Access Critical Friends regularly (at least annually, preferably 2-3 times a year)

Risk Management	
Outcomes & Benefits Management	

Figure 2: Ghanvey Magnificent Matrix cut out. LifeCycle Phase Four: Cruise. Activity Domains – Capability Management

This Ghanvey Magnificent Matrix cut out is a sample of the sorts of tasks that might appear in the Capability Management Activity Domain, in Phase Four: Cruise. Your own project might look quite different.

Your turn:

ACTIVITY

In the cut out below from the Ghanvey Magnificent Matrix, dot point the tasks you need to complete in Capability Management, during Phase Four: Cruise.

THE GHANVEY MAGNIFICENT MATRIX

Activity Domains	Phase Four: Cruise
	Phase Goal: Keep project stable and tracking to target
Governance	
Financial Management	
Stakeholder Engagement	
Capability Management	
Risk Management	
Outcomes & Benefits Management	

Ghanvey LifeCycle Phase One *Cruise*

Risk Management

The Cruise phase is the most dangerous time for a project and the most likely phase in which a project will go off track. There's always a lot going on in the life of a social policy and program professional, so when this particular 3P roll-out looks like it's set up and on its way, it's normal to retreat from actively managing, monitoring and supporting it. Just because you might be taking a little breather, though, that doesn't mean that risk takes a break. **Risk is always there. It doesn't take breaks or holidays**.

It's not all bad, folks. Risk is about threats, yes; that's sometimes called downside risk. Risk is also about opportunities, otherwise known as upside risk.

Now, back to real life on the ground in a 3P roll-out. If you have a program or project that is funded across four years or more, your wider environmental context may undergo seismic shifts during the Cruise phase. Your risk responsibility is to be scanning the environment to guide the big picture. If you're a team of one, that means it's up to you. If you have a steering committee, this is what you put to them for guidance. For example:

- change of ministers in a reshuffle
- change of government (federal, state or local)
- policy announcement
- commencement of a Royal Commission in a different program area
- change of board chair
- change of board members
- change of senior leadership
- organisation merger

Any one of these changes can have a negative or positive impact on your roll-out, depending on what else is happening. One project I supported a couple of years ago in a state government program was trying to stretch its funding, as it needed to cover a pre-service component of the funded service that had not been anticipated. During LifeCycle Phase Three, the project team discovered this pre-service component was essential if the clients were to successfully complete the funded program. During Phase Four: Cruise, the project team was on the lookout for how to fill that gap. The Federal Government announced a program that covered the pre-service piece. A few phone calls and a bit of paperwork later, and that team had a partnership with the Federal Government agency and an end-to-end service for the clients. This is a great example of upside risk that the team had identified as a gap, then scanned the wider environment for a solution to, then facilitated that solution to happen.

I'm pretty sure we could cite other examples of these changes negatively impacting our projects, especially elections that throw up a change of government. New policy directions can mean 3P roll-outs are hastily brought to a close. The only upside of this downside is that it's predictable! Almost all the dot points above have relatively long lead times but it's extraordinary how many 3P roll-out teams don't plan for them. All it takes is to set aside a meeting to discuss the four simple risk questions. "What are they?" I hear you ask.

Remember in Chapter 4 we talked about the four simple risk questions? It was a while ago, so let's do a retake.

Ghanvey LifeCycle Phase One   Cruise   *Cruise*

Simple Downside Risk Questions

1. What can go wrong?
2. What is the likelihood that this could go wrong?
3. What would be the impact (i.e., ripple effect across the Activity Domains) if this did go wrong?
4. What would we do if this happened?

Simple Upside Risk Questions

1. What could work better?
2. What is the likelihood that this could happen?
3. What would be the impact if that happened?
4. How do we facilitate that happening?

As you enter Phase Four: Cruise, it is critically important that you have this discussion across the Activity Domains. Even if you had the discussion in Phase One: Post-Budget Planning, put it on the agenda again twice a year and make sure your responses are up to date.

If you've had an organisational change, your governance structure may no longer be realistic or relevant. That's a governance risk. Earlier, I talked about staff coming and going and how this presents a risk for the team's capability in driving the project forward. In Chapter 6, we saw how financial management can be negatively impacted by service provider performance. These are all risks that need to be acknowledged and responded to.

It's nearly always going to be an emergency that triggers the risk action, so keep the risk ball in play during the Cruise phase.

PROJECT / PROGRAM NAME:	
SUCCESS IS:	
Activity Domains	**Phase Four: Cruise**
	Phase Goal: Keep project stable and tracking to target
Governance	
Financial Management	
Stakeholder Engagement	
Capability Management	Tie up loose ends from Phase Three Regularly assess skills on the ground Update capability management plan annually • Organisational capability • Team capability (and succession skills plan) • Service provider capability Provide access to skills uplift for all project staff Access Critical Friends regularly (at least annually, preferably 2-3 times a year)
Risk Management	Tie up loose ends from Phase Three Annual risk discussion against each Activity Domain to identify threats, opportunities and test compliance Update risk response plan annually Update risk register twice annually
Outcomes & Benefits Management	

Figure 3: Ghanvey Magnificent Matrix cut out. LifeCycle Phase Four: Cruise. Activity Domains – Capability Management and Risk Management

This Ghanvey Magnificent Matrix cut out is a sample of the sorts of tasks that might appear in the Risk Management Activity Domain, in Phase Four: Cruise. Your own project might look quite different.

Ghanvey LifeCycle Phase One Cruise   *Cruise*

Your turn:

ACTIVITY

In the cut out below from the Ghanvey Magnificent Matrix, dot point the tasks you need to complete in Risk Management, during Phase Four: Cruise.

THE GHANVEY MAGNIFICENT MATRIX

PROJECT / PROGRAM NAME:	
SUCCESS IS:	
Activity Domains	**Phase Four: Cruise**
	Phase Goal: Keep project stable and tracking to target
Governance	
Financial Management	
Stakeholder Engagement	
Capability Management	
Risk Management	
Outcomes & Benefits Management	

Outcomes and Benefits Management

Collecting data and impact evidence is a critical part of the Cruise phase, because you and all your stakeholders will be clamouring to know the reasons for why your solution is working or not. The data you collect will relate to your evaluation framework and measures for success (or KPIs) that your project 'owner' or steering committee agreed to during Phase One. Hopefully, your Critical Friends helped you develop KPIs that are relevant, realistic and that align with your already crystal-clear purpose and objectives. I'll assume that when you agreed on the KPIs, you didn't end up with a long list of data that either you or your service provider have to collect, most of which you won't use.

Collecting data and putting together long reports can be very time-consuming for any team. Way too many times, I've seen long reports filed as soon as they come in with only a cursory glance at the contents. That immediately tells me three things: firstly, the staff member collecting the report doesn't understand why they need to read it and what it's telling them – there's an intersection with capability. Secondly, at least some of the data is not needed. Thirdly, there is not likely to be any plan to evaluate the impact of this program, so the staff member believes it's not important to understand the data. All these are indicators of low effectiveness in a 3P roll-out.

Wake up! Data coming in against agreed KPIs is telling you a valuable story about the relative merits of your project. You'll need to know what that story is to continue to manage the project effectively, i.e., apply the relevant resources into relevant actions. That data will also signal your supporting role. Is anyone lagging who needs support? And you guessed it – that data helps you to report progress to the team, the steering committee and the funder.

Hopefully, some of the reporting you gather for your 3P roll-out will be qualitative. If so, you might look out for examples of best practice to share. Remember to analyse it with an open mind so it can tell you the story it has to offer, rather than the one you want it to tell.

Frequently, when I go into support teams, they tell me most of the 'good' work is outsourced. Sometimes that's the case but mostly it's not. Staff miss golden opportunities, like reading these reports. I know it doesn't seem like the 'real' game, but if you know what you're doing, keeping track of outcomes and benefits during a Cruise phase opens up opportunities for immense stimulation across all the areas of the Activity Domains. You'll be amazed what that can throw up, and how this can be an impressive meeting discussion point for you to raise.

As a quick example, think of a report that is telling you they are way over-subscribed with clients in an innovation project. Their progress target was to service 150 clients, and they've already served 220 clients and have a waiting list for more. What's your response? Just file it away thinking "Fantastic, we need more service providers like that who go the extra mile for no extra money?" Well, you could do, but it might come back to bite you later.

It might be better to be curious and ask yourself a few deeper questions. Those questions might look something like these:

- how do they do that?
- are they providing an adequate service to everyone, or is this now a thinned out, quite different service than the one we envisaged?

- how are we going to demonstrate the benefits we've articulated if the service no longer aligns with the original plan?
- are they going to ask for more money?
- should we add something about service demand to our data collection?

These sorts of questions drive straight to the heart of the outcomes and benefits to be derived from the project. That simple report has raised a hornet's nest of issues that run across governance, financial management, stakeholder engagement, risk and, of course, outcomes and benefits.

To keep it contained here, I'm just going to broadly cover one more element of outcomes and benefits management during the Cruise phase. The 3P roll-out team and the steering committee, if there is one, need to be confident that the activities on the ground will actually result in delivering the desired outcomes.

If you have even a sneaking suspicion that the activities you have commissioned are not going to deliver the outcomes you desire, you're going to have to put your thinking cap on and come up with a solution that allows you to pivot back to the right direction. Being in the Cruise phase doesn't mean everything is locked in and can't be changed. It means quite the opposite. Everything needs to be regularly assessed to make sure it *will* deliver the outcomes and provide the benefits that were intended. If any single element looks like it's not taking you towards that vision, move it, shake it and set it right.

When you're in the middle of a 3P roll-out, it's pretty tricky to remain objective, so the Cruise phase is a good time to call in your Critical Friends, as they're independent and can ask questions and challenge your assumptions. It's very important to have regular, objective assessments. I encourage clients to be self-aware, join dots and be curious, but I don't encourage teams to formally self-assess their own progress. Objectivity is key to a balanced assessment and anyone on a team is way too close to the roll-out to achieve an objective state of mind. Having said that, project teams should always be aware of where they are up to in any given LifeCycle phase. For formal progress assessment, build that pool of Critical Friends to call on, always start with purpose and be outcomes-oriented.

Critical Friend training is included as part of a subscription to the Ghanvey digital library. If that's the direction you want to go in, check it out at **3pda.com.au/ghanvey/**.

THE GHANVEY MAGNIFICENT MATRIX

PROJECT / PROGRAM NAME:	
SUCCESS IS:	

Activity Domains	Phase Four: Cruise
	Phase Goal: Keep project stable and tracking to target
Governance	
Financial Management	
Stakeholder Engagement	
Capability Management	Tie up loose ends from Phase Three Regularly assess skills on the ground Update capability management plan annually 　■ Organisational capability 　■ Team capability (and succession skills plan) 　■ Service provider capability Provide access to skills uplift for all project staff Access Critical Friends regularly (at least annually, preferably 2-3 times a year)
Risk Management	Tie up loose ends from Phase Three Annual risk discussion against each Activity Domain to identify threats, opportunities and test compliance Update risk response plan annually Update risk register twice annually
Outcomes & Benefits Management	Tie up loose ends from Phase Three Collect data Analyse data Map out the data story Revise resource allocation if data directs

Figure 4: Ghanvey Magnificent Matrix cut out. LifeCycle Phase Four: Cruise. Activity Domains – Capability Management, Risk Management and Outcomes and Benefits Management

This Ghanvey Magnificent Matrix cut out is a sample of the sorts of tasks that might appear in the Outcomes and Benefits Management Activity Domain, in Phase Four: Cruise. Your own project might look quite different.

Ghanvey LifeCycle Phase One Cruise *Cruise*

Your turn:

ACTIVITY

In the cut out below from the Ghanvey Magnificent Matrix, dot point the tasks you need to complete in Outcomes and Benefits Management, during Phase Four: Cruise.

THE GHANVEY MAGNIFICENT MATRIX

PROJECT / PROGRAM NAME:	
SUCCESS IS:	
	Phase Four: Cruise
Activity Domains	**Phase Goal: Keep project stable and tracking to target**
Governance	
Financial Management	
Stakeholder Engagement	
Capability Management	
Risk Management	
Outcomes & Benefits Management	

Transition to LifeCycle Phase Five

The end of LifeCycle Phase Four: Cruise arises when the funding period is coming to an end. For a two-year (or longer) roll-out, this would be about eight to twelve months before the finish line. For a project roll-out that's fewer than two years in duration, it would be around three to six months before the funding ends.

When Phase Five is approaching, it's time to decide whether to close the program or go back to the funder and ask for another term. This decision must be made clearly and decisively for the benefit of all stakeholders.

Once you're clear about the direction of Phase Five for your 3P roll-out, call the other Critical Friends to help with the transition assessment. Even if you've decided to wind up, you'll need to make sure you enter Phase Five in the best possible shape so you can achieve your desired outcome.

Conclusion

LifeCycle Phase Four is where you'll see your 3P results taking shape. Active **managing, monitoring, supporting and reporting** throughout this phase will reward you with low risk and amplified outcomes. Analyse reports and work with the Activity Domains to keep your project stable and tracking to target. As always, keep your Critical Friends close and use a consistent approach, because **consistency is the key to success**.

Ghanvey LifeCycle Phase One Cruise *Cruise*

Chapter 10: Key Messages

1. Cruising needs focus and attention for serious managing, monitoring, supporting and reporting.

2. There will continue to be wrinkles to iron out. Expect them and learn from them.

3. Stay vigilant and focused.

4. Call your Critical Friends to help you regularly assess progress against the Activity Domains because things can change fast.

5. Risk is always there; it doesn't take breaks or holidays.

6. Only collect relevant data you're going to use.

7. Analyse the data as it comes in so you can continue to direct resources to relevant actions that will take you towards your goal.

8. Consistency is the key to success.

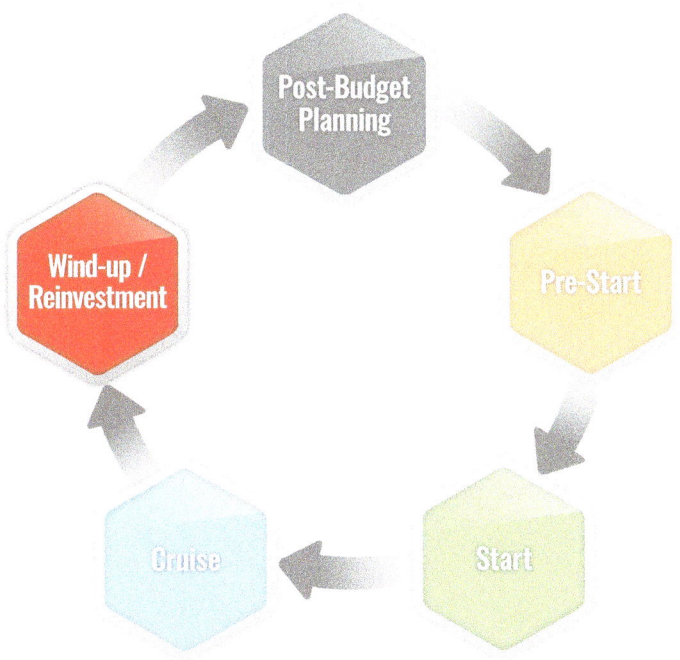

CHAPTER 11

Ghanvey LifeCycle Phase Five:
Wind-up/Reinvestment

Introduction

The Wind-up/Reinvestment Phase is all about managing the final stage of the current funding period, whether that involves closing the project down or going for another term.

Once again, the Activity Domains will be your best friend, backing you up, always there and so reliable. In this chapter, we'll work through the different ways to sync LifeCycle Phase Five and the Activity Domains for both wind-up and reinvestment.

Whichever way you're heading with your 3P-roll out, it needs to be planned and well executed, because you're running with two phases simultaneously: Cruise, because you're still delivering the initiative at this time; and Wind-up/Reinvestment. Winding up still carries a lot of potential risk if not properly managed. Going for continuation puts a spotlight on preparing a new budget proposal. Either way, LifeCycle Phase Five presents an enormous opportunity for learning that should be embraced with a big bear hug. It's not the time to switch off and just let things look after themselves.

It might seem counterintuitive, but many of the elements needed for both choices are the same:

- data collection and analysis
- assessing outcomes achievement
- assessing benefits attainment
- confirming leftover risk
- assessing project performance

Yes, it's a hive of activity. If you aspire to be a proactive, efficient and effective organisation, or (at least) team, then all of these items need to be completed. This is where internal skills, combined with some independent and objective Critical Friends, are once again so important. Most smaller projects that can't quite stretch to a formal evaluation (i.e., a paid evaluation with an expert) can still perform a useful analysis internally, if they know what they're doing.

Analysis of both the project's performance and the team's performance in managing the project will need to

Ghanvey LifeCycle Phase One Wind-up / Reinvestment

be completed if you're seeking continuous improvement and want to be identified as credible and reliable. Credible, reliable and competent are attractive qualities for most funders. In time, I'm guessing these sorts of assessments will become mandatory requirements for funding, so it's probably best to start building your skills and practice now.

In this chapter, I'm going to focus on assessing performance of the project management function rather than on evaluation. I strongly recommend some sort of evaluation of every social purpose project, to learn from what happened in the course of it. An evaluation should be independent and objective, so if you're in charge of a small project with no funds to outsource, this is one of those times you should call in your Critical Friends to help. I'm going to leave evaluation before I've even started on it, now. There are plenty of publications and resources that can inform you about evaluation and I don't feel the need to add to that collection.

Given that there are so many common elements between wind-up and reinvestment, it seems sensible to cover them in one section. In this chapter, I'll provide an overview of Stakeholder Engagement and Risk Management before going into more detail about Outcomes and Benefits Management. Finally, I'll move onto a quick overview of the actions that distinguish a close down and provide some tips for reinvestment.

Ending the Funded Period

Whether you're winding up or reinvesting, you're preparing for the end of the current funding period. That funded period had a defined project, with desired outcomes that were designed to solve a problem. You need to find out now if your solution worked and to what extent it did. If your project is one to two years long, then LifeCycle Phase Five will kick in about three to six months before the end. If the project is three to four years, then you might start this phase about eight months or more from the end, depending on when your new budget proposal is due.

Working the Activity Domains in Phase Five

Activity Domains	Phase Five: Wind-up/Reinvest
	Phase Goal: Analyse, evaluate and learn
Governance	
Financial Management	
Stakeholder Engagement	
Capability Management	
Risk Management	
Outcomes & Benefits Management	

Figure 1: Ghanvey Magnificent Matrix cut out. LifeCycle Phase Five: Wind Up/Reinvestment

Wind-up / Reinvestment

There is rich learning to be had from assessing how well you managed any given project across the six Activity Domains, so you can go forward with reduced risk and amplified outcomes. The project management function is rarely evaluated on the ground, but in my experience, it's a common cause of project problems and failure. The effects of gaps in the project management function are many: time blowouts, budget problems, struggling service providers and disenchanted stakeholders, to name but a few.

Keeping the focus on consistent management across the six Activity Domains ensures that the strategic initiative delivery continues to be on track and the end of the funded project is managed effectively. Let's take a closer look at some Phase Five actions in a selection of Activity Domains.

Stakeholder Engagement

As a quick recap, stakeholder engagement is about knowing your stakeholders really well, understanding the way their role changes across the LifeCycle phases and tailoring communication in a way that is meaningful to them.

If a project has been managed successfully, stakeholder needs and concerns will have been mapped in Phase One and checked for changes during the transition to each new LifeCycle phase, including transition to the Wind-up/Reinvestment phase. There will also be evidence of tailored communication with the different stakeholder groups or categories, and the timing of the communication will have been relevant to their respective levels of participation. In other words, communication has prepared stakeholders to play their part at the right time, in the right way and in the right place.

By the time you arrive at Phase Five, your focus for stakeholder engagement is about seeking their support for reinvestment or supporting them to learn to live without you. The actions needed to support either approach may be similar, like focus groups or training seminars.

If reinvestment is the plan, focus groups can be used to get feedback from stakeholders about where they perceive the value in the initiative and how it could be improved. Clear communication is going to be vital because you don't want to be raising expectations that you have no control over. The key messages might run along these lines:

- we value this initiative and thank you for participating
- if you found the project valuable, can you help us prepare to get funding for another term?
- we can't guarantee we'll get the funding

If closing down is the way forward, feedback about stakeholder experience is still important. It might feed into a different iteration of this initiative at another time. Focus groups can also be an opportunity to educate particular stakeholder categories who may plan to take the initiative forward themselves. Show them how to put a robust funding proposal together.

A seminar or round table might also be a valuable inclusion in Phase Five. "Why would we do that?" I hear you say. "To share best practice and preliminary evaluation data with the people who collected if for you," is my response. I am bemused about why strategic initiatives don't often host these gatherings towards the end of the funded period. Having said that, I'm fully aware that teams can be busier than usual at this time because they're rolling out LifeCycle Phase Four and Five simultaneously, even if they don't realise it. Nevertheless, these stakeholder gatherings

Ghanvey LifeCycle Phase One Wind-up / Reinvestment

can add massive value to continuous improvement for the team, the organisation and the stakeholders. Too often I hear, "We're not ready to share the data, because it hasn't been evaluated." That's not good enough, in my book. That formal evaluation will be months away and everyone will have moved on by then.

Leave stakeholders with a sense that something happened, something has changed, and they were a part of it. It's really not that hard. There will be some data to share and some preliminary case studies to showcase, both good and bad. I'm not saying you should share it on the national news, just among the people who participated and helped you collect the data you have. It's simple respect.

Most of all, during Phase Five, especially when it's getting close to the end of the funded period, remember to celebrate your stakeholders. Even the ones who might have given you quite a bit of grief have probably made you lift your performance. I realise it's hard to accept that, but it's often true. Let your stakeholders know, loudly and clearly, that you value them and appreciate their support and participation in your initiative. This might be in the form of an email or letter, a phone call or a cup of coffee. It is so common for this simple acknowledgement to be overlooked in the busyness of collecting data and preparing budget proposals, or just mentally moving on to the next initiative. Even if you get that renewed funding, different people might be participating, so mark a celebration of some kind in your Stakeholder Engagement Activity Domain for LifeCycle Phase Five.

Let's have a look at what stakeholder engagement looks like in the Ghanvey Magnificent Matrix during LifeCycle Phase Five. Remember, this is only part of the action story, because you're also coordinating and implementing actions for stakeholder engagement for the Cruise phase at the same time.

Activity Domains	Phase Five: Wind-up/Reinvest
	Phase Goal: Analyse, evaluate and learn
Governance	
Financial Management	
Stakeholder Engagement	Focus groups to learn stakeholder value Seminar to share data and learnings Dedicated case studies from stakeholders for reinvestment proposal Celebrate stakeholders
Capability Management	
Risk Management	
Outcomes & Benefits Management	

Figure 2: Ghanvey Magnificent Matrix cut out. LifeCycle Phase Five: Wind Up/Reinvestment. Activity Domain – Stakeholder Engagement

This Ghanvey Magnificent Matrix cut out is a sample of the sorts of tasks that might appear in the Stakeholder Engagement and Communication Activity Domain, in Phase Five: Wind Up/Reinvestment. Your own project might look quite different.

Ghanvey LifeCycle Phase One Wind-up / Reinvestment

Your turn:

ACTIVITY

In the cut out below from the Ghanvey Magnificent Matrix, dot point the tasks you need to complete in Stakeholder Engagement and Communication Activity Domain, during Phase Five: Wind Up/Reinvestment.

PROJECT / PROGRAM NAME:

SUCCESS IS:

Activity Domains	Phase Five: Wind-up/Reinvest
	Phase Goal: Analyse, evaluate and learn
Governance	
Financial Management	
Stakeholder Engagement	
Capability Management	
Risk Management	
Outcomes & Benefits Management	

Risk Management

Just because the current project funding is ending, that doesn't mean the risk magically disappears. Nothing changes for LifeCycle Phase Five – risk is still there and wants to play. This is not the time to think you've already made it and can just switch off. Remember, you're still delivering on the initiative during Phase Five, and you still have stakeholders who need to be engaged and money that needs to be allocated and spent. Stay on high alert.

The risk assessment you need to make for Phase Five is similar to those you've done in the transition to each of the LifeCycle phases for the duration of the project. It's about identifying which risks on the risk plan or register are still live, how likely they are to impact the project and what you might do if they happen.

The additional piece needed for Phase Five is to identify what risks will remain at the end of the project, and where they should go after the project ends. If you're going for reinvestment, you might carry them forward with the renewed project. If you close down, you need to get agreement from your governing body or project 'owner', about who will now 'own' that risk and monitor it, going forward. Let's face it, no one really wants to adopt risk, so don't be surprised if people suddenly become unavailable to talk when they realise what it is you have to say. You may need to learn better ambush skills, which is quite tricky in an environment of video conferencing. The Ghanvey library doesn't have a masterclass on that!

A classic risk that plagues social projects (especially when they don't apply a consistent approach like the Ghanvey method) is unspent funds. There are a hundred reasons why money is left over, some of which are legitimate and

Ghanvey LifeCycle Phase One — Wind-up / Reinvestment

many of which relate to poor project management. It is a clear indicator that there's either no standard method for managing projects at this organisation, or, if there is one, it's underdeveloped.

A common resolution of this financial risk is to commit to a number of vague, sector-aligned, existing services to soak up the funds during Phase Five. While there is some benefit to the sector and their clients, it's not serving the project outcomes. If that project was part of a sector reform program, then the reform isn't going to be realised any time soon. Like so many social sector initiatives, that reform will lag and drag its way to a compromised outcome.

As I mentioned earlier, the project management function is rarely evaluated, except in really big reviews and inquiries. That reform program, where the unspent funds were thrown out the door for different purposes, ends with a full financial acquittal, and that's that. It is not analysed, so there is no learning, when the truth is that the team had a poor financial management approach as well as poor overall capability for social purpose project management. The desired outcomes are not met. That same team will go on to manage other strategic initiatives in exactly the same way. How do I express in writing the sound of my head exploding?

Exhale…

Can we all please acknowledge that this type of approach is actually failure? It is a failure of the project management function, which, in turn, negatively impacts financial management, capability management, risk management, and outcomes and benefits management. Please stop using it! If you want to progress social change, this is definitely one of those things you'll need to let go. Adopting the Ghanvey method is a solution right before your eyes. Please, please,

please work your way through the activities in this book and/or subscribe to the Ghanvey digital library for social purpose project management, where dedicated learning modules and masterclasses will help you to lift your game.

Find it here: **3pda.com.au/ghanvey/**

Okay, going on, continued risk might exist if a service provider has been granted an extension to meet their targets, beyond the life of the project. Hard to believe, but it happens. The project team might dissolve, and no one is left to manage, monitor and support the service provider to finish. You would need to identify someone to 'own' and manage the service provider through to their contract end. After all, this service provider has already been identified as struggling, so if you abandon them, the extension probably won't help anyway. If it's a large provider, there may also be a gap in performance data that needs to be filled, and it might even change the entire narrative, which could be missed if no one is allocated the job of analysing and interpreting this late data. The continuing chain of impact might include a negative impact on vulnerable clients that you will repeat because you didn't learn from all the project data. The chain of impact could keep going further, but I'm pretty sure you've got the message. Identify and resolve risky project leftovers to make sure you understand what happened in this project and can take the learnings into your next one.

At the end of the day, it is always best to try to resolve risk by the end of the funded period so you can save the time and energy it would take to house it somewhere else. When you do that, the resolution should serve the project outcomes, because every action you take for this 3P roll-out is directed at achieving the goal.

Ghanvey LifeCycle Phase One   *Wind-up / Reinvestment*

THE GHANVEY MAGNIFICENT MATRIX

PROJECT / PROGRAM NAME:	
SUCCESS IS:	
	Phase Five: Wind-up/Reinvest
Activity Domains	**Phase Goal: Analyse, evaluate and learn**
Governance	
Financial Management	
Stakeholder Engagement	Focus groups to learn stakeholder value Seminar to share data and learnings Dedicated case studies from stakeholders for reinvestment proposal Celebrate stakeholders
Capability Management	
Risk Management	Update risk plan against the Activity Domains Update risk register Identify unresolved risk Hand over unresolved risk
Outcomes & Benefits Management	

Figure 3: Ghanvey Magnificent Matrix cut out. LifeCycle Phase Five: Wind Up/Reinvestment. Activity Domains – Stakeholder Engagement and Risk Management

This Ghanvey Magnificent Matrix cut out is a sample of the sorts of tasks that might appear in the Risk Management Activity Domain, in Phase Five: Wind Up/Reinvestment. Your own project might look quite different.

Rock your Roll Out

Your turn:

> **ACTIVITY**
>
> In the cut out below from the Ghanvey Magnificent Matrix, dot point the tasks you need to complete in Risk Management, during Phase Five: Wind Up/Reinvestment.

THE GHANVEY MAGNIFICENT MATRIX

PROJECT / PROGRAM NAME:	
SUCCESS IS:	

Activity Domains	Phase Five: Wind-up/Reinvest
	Phase Goal: Analyse, evaluate and learn
Governance	
Financial Management	
Stakeholder Engagement	
Capability Management	
Risk Management	
Outcomes & Benefits Management	

Ghanvey LifeCycle Phase One   Wind-up / Reinvestment

Outcomes & Benefits Management

Outcomes

First things first. How can you tell if you achieved what you set out to achieve? That all depends on the clarity of the outcome statement you confirmed in Phase One: Post-Budget Planning. I'm going to assume your outcomes statement was crystal clear and included the five Ws for the project (why, what, who, where and when), because you followed the method I outlined in Chapter 7 of this book. Your performance indicators for the project hang off that outcome statement; that's why it needs to be absolutely crystal clear and include those five Ws. I know I repeated that line, it's to emphasise its importance. If you need to revise, head back to Chapter 7.

Just in case this is all new and you haven't applied your learning yet, here's a quick re-cap. The well-designed outcome statement enables you to identify clear performance indicators for the project. If you have a broad outcome statement like 'To continue to reduce substance abuse' or 'To increase audience numbers,' it doesn't land you anywhere in particular at any time in particular. It won't focus your resources and it definitely won't achieve anything in particular. The first questions a funder would ask about these sorts of outcome statements are: what substances – everything? If you get two more audience members than last year, is that a win?

If you have a crystal-clear outcomes statement it will tell you what success looks like for this project, because it will include what the end goal is, where the focus of activity will be and what the timeline will be. 'Reducing overuse of pharmaceutical drugs by 20 percent over three years,' or 'Increasing annual audience numbers by 20 percent each year for three years,' provides a lot more focus, and all the key stakeholders will understand what they're aiming for.

Let's have a look at a more detailed example. In Chapter 4, I outlined a case study of an organisation I worked with that transformed itself through a well-designed outcomes statement. It started out with a broad statement: 'Collecting samples of SPM disease (a made-up disease name) for clinical research,' and almost fell apart because the statement had no end goal. The focus closed in on activities for activities' sake. They couldn't tell if they were successful, because there was no picture of success to compare their performance to. Their transformation as an organisation started with a clear outcome statement that went something like this: 'Our aim is to assemble a world class collection of annotated samples of SPM disease, collected in X place, that researchers can access within 48 hours of request, by June 2022.' This clear statement not only provided focus to their activities, it also enabled a set of simple and clear performance indicators to be identified that could then be used to test whether they were successful.

If you were that organisation, you would have established some simple and useful performance indicators in Phase One: Post-Budget Planning that align to a picture of success. They might have looked something like this:

- the collection is world class
- the collection size and distribution across sub-streams is known
- the collection is fully annotated
- the collection is relevant to researchers
- research requests can be consistently met within 48 hours

Ghanvey LifeCycle Phase One — Wind-up / Reinvestment

During Phase One, you would also have figured out how you would assess these indicators, like establishing the benchmark criteria for a world class sample collection. During Phase Five, you analyse the results to bring the story of relative success to the foreground. For example, have you demonstrated that your sample collection now meets all the criteria for a world class collection? To demonstrate whether the collection is relevant to researchers, you would need to show results from a survey or focus groups with researchers, that tells you their needs and illustrates how the collection meets those needs. Those surveys or focus groups might have been conducted late in Phase Four or early in Phase Five. You get the idea.

The answers that come up during Phase Five analysis should be no surprise if you're using the Ghanvey method. This is because you will have been cross-checking your Activity Domains during each LifeCycle phase to make sure your actions were tracking in alignment with your desired outcome. Having done that, you would have found problems early on and fixed them quickly.

If a funder asks, "Were you successful in meeting your outcomes?", they want a "yes" or "no". Like I said earlier in the book, somewhat controversially, if you were partially successful, then the answer is "no". But "It's not that black and white", you plead, and I agree, but I'm trying to give you a funder's perspective here. When the answer is "no", it tells me two things: you didn't scope the project effectively (you've promised too much on a shoestring budget), or you lack capability for social purpose project management. Either way, outcomes like this can be fixed and turned around. The problem is not that you're intrinsically incompetent. By lifting your capability and your consistency in approach to social purpose project management through using the

Ghanvey method, you'll be able to answer a very confident "yes" to your funders and other stakeholders alike, in future.

If this book is resonating with you, a subscription to the Ghanvey digital library of learning modules, masterclasses and Critical Friend training will prove a valuable investment to transform your outcomes. Find it here: **3pda.com.au/ghanvey/**

Data Story

Given that Outcomes and Benefits Management in Phase Five is about pulling together all the data you've collected along the way, I think it's a good idea to have a close look at what I call the 'data story'. I have to admit I'm not the world's greatest data head, but I recognise its utility for telling a story. The first thing to emphasise here is the use of both quantitative (the numbers) and qualitative (the people) data together, to tell a complete story. If you have only figures, then you'll only have one side of the story. You could be missing vital information that supports interpretation of the figures. For example, you could report that you met the target of 250 units of service this quarter and leave it at that. An emerging trend among the clients receiving those services is that they are increasingly wanting referrals to training. If this bit is not reported, then the desired training services won't be able to grow or tailor their offerings to meet this emerging demand, and the client group will miss out on an opportunity to better self-manage their lives.

The data story is about how well this project solved a pressing social need and derived a range of benefits from doing so. The story will be put together with data from performance indicators, set against the project outcomes statement, benefits measures (discussed below) and from the Activity Domains.

Ghanvey LifeCycle Phase One *Wind-up / Reinvestment*

The cause of problems is likely to be found somewhere across the Activity Domains: a clunky governance structure that didn't facilitate fast decision-making; poor financial management that meant funds weren't fully applied to the project; capability gaps across the organisation and the team; poor risk identification or lack of focus on outcomes and benefits management across all the LifeCycle phases. How many data measures have you seen for these sorts of things? "None," you say? Me neither. I don't think I've ever seen them, but they're common and fundamental reasons for social programs and projects not quite meeting the mark. Assessing these sorts of measures is usually reserved for the major Review or Royal Commission that comes after all the other, standard data measures have blown up.

Once you've got your relevant and useful dataset across the project's performance indicators and Activity Domains, you need to analyse it and let it tell the story it has to tell, rather than the story you would like it to tell. It can be a bit uncomfortable sometimes, but if you take a continuous improvement mindset, then you'll know where to do things differently next time. Without that learning mindset, you'll end up making the same mistakes all the time. I realise a lot of organisations are somewhat terrified of their funder and believe if they admit any sort of failure they'll be cut off without any further questions. This can inhibit their honesty.

Firstly, to funders: get real, banana peel. If an organisation can identify where it went wrong, it means it will be stronger and an even safer investment for your money next time around. Secondly, to the funded, it's time to educate the funders and explicitly show them the benefits of consistency and learning. If you show them you're using the Ghanvey method to manage your strategic social purpose initiatives across LifeCycle phases that are synchronised with actions across a set of standard Activity Domains, you'll blow their minds. How much fun would that be?!

Benefits Attainment

Benefits are the "So what?" part of the outcome equation. It's about knowing what difference the project made. To be able to tell whether the anticipated benefits happened and made the positive difference your project objectives anticipated they would, they need to be set up from the start of the project in a way that is measurable. That will have been done or at least confirmed during Phase One: Post-Budget Planning.

I've seen some pretty wild looking benefits in my time, with tenuous links to the project at best, and no links to the project, at worst. Here's a quick way of zoning in on whether a benefit has a link to the project or not. Consider that, if you didn't do this project, then these things wouldn't happen. On the flip side, these things only happen because you did the project. You can't say that a small local project to bring communities together with culturally inclusive activities has a benefit of world peace. To start with, you'd have to figure out how you would define and measure world peace, and then you'd have to demonstrate that world peace only happened because of your project. Okay, that's extreme, but let me tell you, I've seen stated benefits that are not far off this kind of stretch.

Measuring benefits is all about comparing: comparing what is happening at the beginning of the project to what will happen after the project is introduced or completed. For that beautiful community project, you can anticipate a benefit as being a contribution to reduced, culturally motivated, local crime. So, to include this as a benefit, you'd need to check that you could measure the level of that sort

Ghanvey LifeCycle Phase One *Wind-up / Reinvestment*

of crime before and after you finish the project. If you follow the Ghanvey method, you would already have a sense of whether the benefits you anticipated were starting to kick in by the time you reach Phase Five. I know you're going to be extra busy in the Phase Five, so instead of starting from scratch to build the benefits profile, I designed the Ghanvey method to support you to do part of the work in each LifeCycle Phase along the way.

In Phase Five, you need to collect all the evidence and see if it tells you that the benefits are starting to be realised. If the benefits you anticipated don't happen, it's important you find the reason. There may be hidden external factors you didn't have on your risk plan. Conversely, there may be benefits happening you didn't anticipate and haven't measured. These sorts of things are always exciting to find, like partnerships or an alliance between culturally specific organisations in the community who have decided to work together for the first time, specifically because of this project. Just because you didn't anticipate it doesn't mean you can't brag about it. Publicise these sorts of wins as much as you like. Just make sure it happened *because* of your project before you shout it from the rooftops.

A lot of benefits in social purpose projects are only fully realised after the end of the project. This is why you need to be very cautious about the specific benefits you identify for the project. For example, let's pick up the pretend example we used in Chapter 7, Ghanvey LifeCycle Phase One: Post-Budget Planning, about safe houses for victims of family violence.

Project objective:

- to provide 100 safe houses, for victims of family violence and their children, statewide, by June 2025.

Inputs:

- build 70 new stock
- lease 30 new stock
- establish real-time statewide stock availability register for relevant services to access
- establish wraparound services for tenants

Outputs:

- 100 new safe houses available to women and children affected by family violence
- a safe house availability register that service providers can access in real time
- wraparound service access to safe house occupants

Outcomes:

- safe house availability now meets demand
- stock availability register saves time and increases safety options available to service providers
- wraparound services support participants to stabilise their lives before they leave the safe house

Benefits (so what?):

- increases efficiency of allocation through reducing time taken to find a safe house option
- reduces risk to clients affected by family violence
- increases service quality for clients

Let's have a look at how actions in Phase Five might come together for Outcomes and Benefits Management, remembering these actions are in addition to the Cruise phase actions that continue simultaneously.

Ghanvey LifeCycle Phase One — Wind-up / Reinvestment

THE GHANVEY MAGNIFICENT MATRIX

PROJECT / PROGRAM NAME:	
SUCCESS IS:	

	Phase Five: Wind-up/Reinvest
Activity Domains	**Phase Goal: Analyse, evaluate and learn**
Governance	
Financial Management	
Stakeholder Engagement	Focus groups to learn stakeholder value Seminar to share data and learnings Dedicated case studies from stakeholders for reinvestment proposal Celebrate stakeholders
Capability Management	
Risk Management	Update risk plan against the Activity Domains Update risk register Identify unresolved risk Hand over unresolved risk
Outcomes & Benefits Management	Finalise data collection Analyse data collection Prepare data story (maybe through case studies) Confirm outcomes Confirm benefits Identify outcomes and benefits gaps or problems Identify unexpected wins

Figure 4: Ghanvey Magnificent Matrix cut out. LifeCycle Phase Five: Wind Up/Reinvestment. Activity Domains – Stakeholder Engagement, Risk Management and Outcomes & Benefits Management

This Ghanvey Magnificent Matrix cut out is a sample of the sorts of tasks that might appear in the Outcomes & Benefits Management Activity Domain, in Phase Five: Wind Up/Reinvestment. Your own project might look quite different.

Your turn:

> **ACTIVITY**
>
> In the cut out below from the Ghanvey Magnificent Matrix, dot point the tasks you need to complete in Outcomes & Benefits Management, during Phase Five: Wind Up/Reinvestment.

PROJECT / PROGRAM NAME:	
SUCCESS IS:	
	Phase Five: Wind-up/Reinvest
Activity Domains	**Phase Goal: Analyse, evaluate and learn**
Governance	
Financial Management	
Stakeholder Engagement	
Capability Management	
Risk Management	
Outcomes & Benefits Management	

Ghanvey LifeCycle Phase One   Wind-up / Reinvestment

Winding Up

Wind-up needs to be planned. Don't think this 3P roll-out will naturally fizzle once the money stops. Projects don't wind up on their own. There's a lot to do before and after the money dries up.

There will be a series of key decisions that need to be authorised during Phase Five, which means the governing body or project 'owner' will need to stay across delivery of the initiative, which is still happening, as well as specific issues associated with project closure. These might include some of the issues outlined below:

1. *Governance* – may need additional meeting(s) to authorise series of closure specific decisions.

2. *Financial management* – what to do with money or assets left over?

3. *Stakeholder Engagement* – how to appropriately celebrate their participation and walk away?

4. *Capability Management* – how to retain sufficient capability on the ground to continue initiative delivery until the cut-off date (i.e., retain staff)? How to learn from the project management experience?

5. *Risk Management* – how to transition the program to a different distribution (if relevant)? Online resources and/or presence to remain 'live' or not?

6. *Outcomes and Benefits Management* – will the final report be public, available to stakeholder participants? How will the report learnings be incorporated into future projects?

Reinvestment

Reinvestment also needs to be planned and it's going to be intense. By reinvestment, I mean the project is going to continue for another term, or at least that's what you hope and plan will happen. Of course, if you don't get the funding to continue, you'll need to revert to a close down quickly.

The reinvestment phase is very much in a budget proposal space, so here are some tips.

For reinvestment, your proposal will need to demonstrate ongoing need, show how this approach is still the best solution to meeting that need and provide a robust rationale for costings. You'll need to check in again with your strategic environment as that may have shifted.

In the current funding term, your area might have benefited from being a spotlight reform space because the work was in response to a Royal Commission and there was a pressing need to demonstrate that the recommendations were met. By the time you apply for another funding term, the spotlight (and the money) may well be moving on to respond to a different Royal Commission or major Review. That's going to mean a very different budget proposal, one that needs to align to the shifted environment.

The Reinvestment Budget Proposal

Writing a proposal that shows 10 pages of evidence about why your project is fabulous probably won't get you any money. I mean that with all due respect to the time and effort taken to prepare that proposal. Can I be bluntly honest here? It won't be read. No one really understands the details as much as you do. The funders don't live and breathe it like you do, and they don't need to. In about 95 percent of cases, they just want to know the key points.

Ghanvey LifeCycle Phase One *Wind-up / Reinvestment*

Using the Ghanvey method to structure a proposal (and subsequently the project roll- out) will help the lights go on for funders. It removes a lot of guesswork and is one of the best mechanisms I've seen for getting what you want.

To support your reinvestment proposal, you'll need to collect and collate all your data about success measures (including the budget) and tell a story about what you learnt and how it will inform a better, more effective and efficient 'Mark 2'. Part of this story will need to include a clear, structured and consistent approach to implementation, as well as demonstrating your team's capability for sustaining another term.

The story you tell will need to comprise feedback from your stakeholders where appropriate, especially service providers and clients. Try focus groups to get some feedback about how best to direct the service or program, should another term be funded.

Once you've collated all your material for the reinvestment proposal, you may find that, while the purpose remains the same, the objectives and scope may be a little different. This is normal. There is nothing quite like a V1 roll-out to help you refine needs and shape directions for V2.

Many budget proposals are template-based, meaning the funder has a set way for you to apply. This is great for overall efficiency, but the embedded questions, often set by financial analysts, don't usually make sense to social purpose programs and projects. For anyone filling in one of those templates, it can be a trying time. Let me give you some tips across two areas that seem to bring the most grief.

When a template asks you to describe the project in summary, it means it wants pithy answers to these sorts of questions:

- What is the need?
- What are you asking us to buy?
- What are we getting for the money?
- How does it align with our priorities?
- Will our investment resolve the need?

The top-level answer should be pithy and hit them in the face, so to speak.

> "This project is an investment of $X over two years to reduce response times for XYZ service. Response times are a problem because: people die if they wait too long; there are statutory timelines... The investment will purchase: staff; IT systems; skills training... The first term of funding reduced response times by 15% in the context of 19% growth in clients. Anticipating continued growth of service numbers to 25%, the goal this time is to reduce response times by a further 10% to meet statutory accountability."

Six lines provide all the information the funder analyst needs to know, and they can get across it all in less than one minute. You can fill in the details later in the proposal.

Another part of budget proposals that social policy and programs teams find tricky, in my experience, is when they are asked to comment on the "deliverability" of their proposal. "What are they talking about? We've already covered everything, haven't we? We always have to repeat everything in these templates." Sound familiar? Deliverability is more of an infrastructure term, but it's making its way into social purpose arenas with some force, so listen carefully.

Deliverability in social project settings means, **"How can we be confident that your team can implement this project**

Ghanvey LifeCycle Phase One Wind-up / Reinvestment

successfully?" In other words, the funder wants to know if you're a safe set of hands for their investment.

"Well, are you?" I ask.

"We've already done this once and achieved a lot and we've told them that three times in other sections."

"Your funder understands you've done this before," I respond. "That's history. They want to know about the future. What tool are you going to work with to demonstrate you've thought about the future?"

At this point, I can see brains ticking over, really trying to process the question I just asked.

"Any clues?" they ask sheepishly.

"Well, I'm in love with it," I say with a smile.

"Ohhhh!" The penny's dropped. "The Ghanvey Magnificent Matrix."

"Bullseye!"

If you demonstrate to the funder that you have a plan with LifeCycle phases for the duration and Activity Domains for actions, they will understand you. If you can demonstrate how those Activity Domains sync with the LifeCycles phases, they will love you. Try this:

1. *Governance* – show the anticipated structure and anticipated key roles.

2. *Financial Management* – show the 'architecture' of financial allocation across the LifeCycle phases.

3. *Stakeholder Engagement* – show the map of interests and concerns, even if it's only headline level, and use the

LifeCycle phases to indicate when to expect concerns to flare up.

4. *Capability Management* – demonstrate the skills across the team and how you plan to develop them. Outline a succession plan if key team members leave. Indicate how you learn from all projects.

5. *Risk Management* – show an outline of key risks, identify the LifeCycle phase in which they are likely to arise, and how you might respond accordingly.

6. *Outcomes and Benefits Management* – outline the impact you intend to make and the data you intend to collect to demonstrate this impact. Also, outline your plan to regularly assess and track O&Bs across all the LifeCycles phases.

> ### Box 1: Key points to cover in a detailed budget proposal
>
> 1. What *exactly* is the problem?
> 2. What is your proposed solution?
> 3. What part of the solution are you asking us to invest in?
> 4. What is being purchased with this investment?
> 5. What difference will this investment make?
> 6. How are you going to deliver this project?

Ghanvey LifeCycle Phase One — Wind-up / Reinvestment

You should now be able to see the importance of the Ghanvey method for a structured and consistent approach to managing all manner and size of strategic social programs and projects. The method can be scaled up and down to suit your needs and it applies to everything, from the start to the finish.

Do your organisation and team a favour and subscribe to the Ghanvey digital library of learning modules, masterclasses and Critical Friend training. You'll never look back.

Find it here: **3pda.com.au/ghanvey/**

Conclusion

LifeCycle Phase Five is the time to apply all the resources you can afford on this initiative, because you're running two phases simultaneously. LifeCycle Phase Four: Cruise continues through to the end of the funded period, and LifeCycle Phase Five is introduced as an overlay to determine if you met, or are about to meet, your desired outcome.

All the Activity Domains still need active management through Phase Five. It is an enormous opportunity for learning and continuous improvement. Seek feedback and further support from stakeholders and remember to celebrate their participation. Identify unresolved risk and find a home for any risk you can't resolve before the end.

Outcomes & Benefits Management will take a prominent position during Phase Five. This is the time for bringing together all the data you have collected along the journey, so the story it tells about your relative success in solving the problem you originally identified can come to the surface.

If reinvesting, use your data story and the Ghanvey method to submit a cracking budget proposal.

Phase Five should also be a time for assessing project management performance. In your team, discuss how you performed across each Activity Domain during each LifeCycle phase and call in your Critical Friends to join the discussion. Learn how to do the next project better.

Chapter 11: Key Messages

1. Winding up a funded program or project needs to be planned.
2. Reinvestment of a funded program needs to be planned.
3. Seek feedback from stakeholders and celebrate their participation.
4. Have a plan for unresolved risk.
5. Use your data to tell the story of your outcomes.
6. Only claim benefits that happened because of your project.
7. Create sustainable success and learn from all your 3P roll-outs.

CHAPTER 12
Summary and Conclusion

That's it. That's the Ghanvey method and you've reached the end. It's a bit surreal coming to the end of writing this book and my brain hurts a bit – in a good way. The experience has forced me to be clear and articulate the Ghanvey method in a step-by-step way that I would not normally do so deliberately. It has also forced me to be clear about my own purpose, which is to drive positive social change by supporting sustainable success for social purpose professionals working on the front line of that change.

Social purpose is heavily influenced these days by responding to major Reviews, Inquiries, Audits or Royal Commissions. It's very much 'the new black' for shaping investment. Like I said at the very beginning, investment is investment is investment – and all of it needs to be supported to perform well and achieve goals. The way social purpose professionals work will need to shift to meet this new agenda. Strategic reform programs, new initiatives, innovation projects and grants programs will be far more common in future years. Social purpose project management skills are critical for responding to this shift. They are the solution to your sustainable success story, going forward.

I think I have one last opportunity to bang on about having access to a consistent and standard method of approaching 3P roll-outs that makes sense to project teams and funders alike, so I'll take it. I, for one, support the sort of approach that is standardised in a way that still reflects the flexibility needed for social purpose, yet also takes it beyond unhelpful compromise. Just like infrastructure, I want to see a playing field where this approach is standard and accepted as the way we do things. I want this sort of consistency so we can keep 3P professionals like you safe, meet the outcomes our projects desire, and drive the social change we need.

This is the picture of sustainable success I want for you, and if you use the Ghanvey method, it's going to get you a lot closer to it.

Best wishes with your future 3P roll-outs.

Estelle O'Callaghan

APPENDIX 1
Glossary of Terms

Ghanvey method – an approach to managing social purpose strategic initiatives, developed by Estelle O'Callaghan, designed to minimise risk and amplify outcomes. The Ghanvey method can be used by government at any level, not-for-profit organisations, philanthropic bodies and corporate social responsibility divisions of businesses.

Lifecycle phases – represent the life journey of the project, from being allocated a budget to ending the funded period. The phases help to organise actions into manageable time chunks in a way that brings focused attention to the specific project needs and ensures those needs are met.

Activity Domains – are the key areas for actions within any given LifeCycle phase. If all Activity Domains are actively managed across the LifeCycle phases, the project is likely to meet its desired outcomes.

Critical Friends – are a pool of people the project team has 'on call' to help with objective assessment. They assess project health at the transition to each new LifeCycle phase and can assist at other times when needed. Critical Friends can be internal (but not working on this particular 3P roll-out) or external. A combination of both is often a good place to land. Critical Friend training is available to subscribers of the Ghanvey Library for Social Purpose Project Management.

Ghanvey Magnificent Matrix – is a valuable and versatile tool that brings together the LifeCycle phases and the Activity Domains. This effectively synchronises the big picture and the detail so you can see the logical flow of your project and better understand the ripple effect of any changes or problems. It enables you to see what is coming up in the next LifeCycle phase, ahead of time. The Ghanvey Magnificent Matrix can also be used to map decisions needed across the project, and as a reporting tool to report on project progress.

3P roll-outs – are roll-outs of strategic initiatives across social purpose **p**olicy, **p**rograms or **p**rojects, literally three 'Ps'.

APPENDIX 2

Social Policy-related Royal Commissions and Inquiries, 2000 to 2019

No.	RC/ Inquiry/ Review	Title	Year	No. of Recommendations	Budget Source	Funding
NATIONAL						
1	RC	Violence, Abuse, Neglect and Exploitation of People with Disability	2019 – present	N/A		
2	RC	Aged Care Quality and Safety	2018 – present	N/A		
3	RC	Child Protection and Youth Detention Systems of the Government of the Northern Territory	2016 – 2017	227	2018/19 Northern Territory State Budget	$248.17M
					2018/19 Federal Budget	$259.6M
4	RC	Institutional Responses to Child Sexual Abuse	2013 – 2017	409	2017/18 Federal Budget	$500M+

No.	RC/ Inquiry/ Review	Title	Year	No. of Recommendations	Budget Source	Funding
VICTORIA						
5	RC	Mental Health	2018 – present	N/A		
6	RC	Family Violence	2016 – 2018	227	2016/17 State Budget	$572M over 2 years
					2017/18 State Budget	$1.9B over 4 years
						$131M child pro-tection services
7	R	Targeting zero: Supporting the Victorian hospital system to eliminate avoidable harm and strengthen quality of care	Oct 2016	60	2017/18 State Budget	$215M Better Safer Care reforms
8	R	Investigation into Perinatal Outcomes at Djerriwarrh Health Services by Professor Euan M Wallace	2016	11	2016/17 State Budget	$369M services and infra-structure
9	I	Protecting Victoria's Vulnerable Children	2012	90	2012/13 State Budget	$80M over five years
QUEENSLAND						
10	CI	Barrett Adolescent Centre	2015 – 2016	6	2016/17 State Budget	$35M over 2 years (?) couldn't find direct match
11	CI	Queensland Child Protection	2012 – 2013	121	2014/15 State Budget	$406M over 5 years

No.	RC/ Inquiry/ Review	Title	Year	No. of Recommendations	Budget Source	Funding
12	CI	Queensland Public Hospitals	2005	7	2006/07 State Budget	$9.7B over 5 years
SOUTH AUSTRALIA						
13	CI	Child Protection Systems	2014 – 2016	260		
14	RC	Report of Independent Education	2012 – 2013	43		Too hard to tell – packaged up with Gonski
15	RC	Kapunda Road	2005	7 (?)	2005/06 State Budget	$68.8M over 4 years
16	CI	Children on the APY Lands	2004 – 2008	46	?	
17	CI	Children in State Care	2004 – 2008	51	2008/09 State Budget	$48.4M over 4 years $7.5M Office of the Director for Public Prosecutions including response the Children in State Care Inquiry

No.	RC/ Inquiry/ Review	Title	Year	No. of Recommendations	Budget Source	Funding
WESTERN AUSTRALIA						
		NIL				
NEW SOUTH WALES						
		NIL				
TASMANIA						
		NIL				

RC – Royal Commission   CI – Commission of Inquiry
PI – Public Inquiry   R – Review

REFERENCE LIST

Asquith, J. (2019). A new world of work for government. *The Mandarin* [online] Available from: https://www.themandarin.com.au/109741-a-new-world-of-work-for-government/ [accessed 31 December 2020].

Australia and New Zealand School of Government (2019). *Why Public Sector Leaders Need to Give Staff Freedom to Cross Boundaries.* [online] Available from: https://www.anzsog.edu.au/resource-library/news-media/why-public-sector-leaders-need-to-give-staff-freedom-to-cross-boundaries [accessed 31 December 2020].

Australia and New Zealand School of Government (2019). *Beyond Outsourcing: How Governments Can Change Their Approach to Contracting Services.* [online] Available from: https://www.anzsog.edu.au/resource-library/research/beyond-outsourcing-how-governments-can-change-their-approach-to-contracting-services [accessed 31 December 2020].

Australian Accounting Research Foundation (2002). *Performance Audit: Auditing Standard AUS 806.* [online] Available from: https://www.auasb.gov.au/admin/file/

content102/c3/AUS806_07-02.pdf. [accessed 31 December 2020].

Australian Public Service Commission (2015). *Learning from Failure: why large government policy initiatives have gone so badly wrong in the past and how the chances of success in the future can be improved.* [online] Canberra: Commonwealth of Australia. Available from: https://www.apsc.gov.au/learning-failure-why-large-government-policy-initiatives-have-gone-so-badly-wrong-past-and-how [accessed 31 December 2020].

Collins, J. (2011). *Good To Great.* 1st ed. New York: HarperCollins.

Collins, J. (2011). *Good To Great and the Social Sectors.* 1st ed. New York: HarperCollins.

Department of Treasury and Finance (2016). *Budget Paper No.2 Strategy and Outlook 2016–2017.* [online] Victoria: Victorian Government. Available from: https://www.dtf.vic.gov.au/previous-budgets/2016-17-state-budget [accessed 31 December 2020].

Department of Treasury and Finance (2019). *Gateway Review process.* [online] Available from: https://www.dtf.vic.gov.au/infrastructure-investment/gateway-review-process [accessed 31 December 2020].

Donaldson, D. (2018). 'Urgent': former secretaries assess public service capability. *The Mandarin* [online] Available from: https://www.themandarin.com.au/88048-urgent-former-secretaries-assess-public-service-capability/ [accessed 31 December 2020].

Donaldson, D. (2016). What 'follow the dollar' powers mean for Victoria's public contracts. *The Mandarin* [online] Available from: https://www.themandarin.com.au/65759-

follow-the-dollar-powers-for-vic-auditor-general-at-last/ [accessed 31 December 2020].

Easton, S. (2019). APS secretaries unveil new online collaboration hub in push to improve policy skills. *The Mandarin* [online] Available from: https://www.themandarin.com.au/110225-aps-secretaries-unveil-new-online-collaboration-hub-in-push-to-improve-policy-skills/ [accessed 31 December 2020].

Easton, S. (2017). Sweeping human services overhaul depends on government stewardship. *The Mandarin* [online] Available from: <https://www.themandarin.com.au/79822-governments-key-stewardship-role-in-a-sweeping-human-services-overhaul/> [accessed 31 December 2020].

Family Violence Reform Implementation Monitor (2018). *Report of the Family Violence Reform Implementation Monitor.* Melbourne: Victorian Government [online] Available from: https://www.fvrim.vic.gov.au/first-report-parliament-1-november-2017 [accessed 31 December 2020].

Family Violence Reform Implementation Monitor (2019). *Report of the Family Violence Reform Implementation Monitor.* Melbourne: Victorian Government [online] Available from: https://www.fvrim.vic.gov.au/second-report-parliament-1-november-2018 [accessed 31 December 2020].

Family Violence Reform Implementation Monitor (2020). *Report of the Family Violence Reform Implementation Monitor.* Melbourne: Victorian Government [online] Available from: https://www.fvrim.vic.gov.au/third-report-parliament-1-november-2019 [accessed 31 December 2020].

Gompertz, W. (2015). *Think Like An Artist.* 1st ed. UK: Penguin Random House.

McLeod, M. (2020). *The Support Report: The changing shape of giving and the significant implications for recipients* Brisbane: JBWere [online] Available from: https://www.jbwere.com.au/content/dam/jbwere/documents/JBWere-Support-Report-2018.pdf [accessed 31 March 2020].

Jenkins, S. (2019). New bill aims to keep Victoria's councils accountable. *The Mandarin* [online] Available from: https://www.themandarin.com.au/110037-new-bill-aims-to-keep-victorias-councils-accountable/ [accessed 31 December 2020].

Jenkins, S. (2019). Queensland public sector needs 'talent'. *The Mandarin* [online] Available from: https://www.themandarin.com.au/109760-queensland-public-sector-needs-talent/ [accessed 31 December 2020].

Katsonis, M. (2019). Rethinking policy capacity, competencies and capabilities. *Australia and New Zealand School of Government* [online] Available from: https://www.anzsog.edu.au/resource-library/research/rethinking-policy-capacity-competencies-and-capabilities [accessed 31 December 2020].

NSW Treasury, 2019. Recurrent Expenditure Assurance Framework. {online] Available at: https://www.treasury.nsw.gov.au/information-public-entities/governance-risk-and-assurance/recurrent-expenditure-assurance-framework [accessed 31 December 2020].

Cook, L., Grove, A., & Klapdor, M. (2019). *Social Security and Welfare: Key Figures, Budget Review 2019-20 Index.* Canberra: Parliament of Australia [online] Available from: https://www.aph.gov.au/About_Parliament/Parliamentary_Departments/Parliamentary_Library/pubs/rp/BudgetReview201920/SocialSecurityWelfare [accessed: 1 December 2020].

Arthur, D. (2015). *What Counts as Welfare Spending?* Canberra: Parliament of Australia[online] Available from: https://www.aph.gov.au/About_Parliament/Parliamentary_Departments/Parliamentary_Library/pubs/rp/rp1516/WelfareSpend [accessed 1 December 2020].

Philanthropy Australia (2020). *Giving in Australia: the fast facts.* [online] Available from: https://www.philanthropy.org.au/tools-resources/fast-facts-and-stats/ [accessed 1 December 2020].

Victorian Auditor General's Office (2018). *Contract Management Capability in DHHS: Service Agreements.* Melbourne: Victorian Government [online] Available from: https://www.audit.vic.gov.au/report/contract-management-capability-dhhs-service-agreements [accessed 31 December 2020].

Victorian Auditor General's Office (2013). *Planning, Delivery and Benefits Realisation of Major Asset Investment: The Gateway Review Process.* Melbourne: Victorian Government [online] Available from: https://www.audit.vic.gov.au/report/planning-delivery-and-benefits-realisation-major-asset-investment-gateway-review-process [accessed 31 December 2020].

van der Voort, H., Koppenjan, J., Heuvelhof, E.T., Lejten, M., Veeneman W. (2011). Competing values in the Management of innovative projects: The Case of the RandstadRail Project. In: Bekkers, V., Edelenbos, J., and Steijn, B. (Eds) *Innovation in the Public sector. Linking Capacity and Leadership.* Basingstoke, UK: Palgrave MacMillan.

ABOUT THE AUTHOR

Estelle O'Callaghan is the founder and Director of 3P Delivery Authority. As a thought leader her mission is to support social purpose professionals to thrive so that together they can make positive social change happen.

Estelle works with governments, statutory authorities, not-for-profit organisations, and is currently reaching further across the sector into philanthropic bodies and corporate social responsibility. She has turned around projects and teams from the brink of despair to sustainable outcomes achievement. She would like to inspire more teams to set themselves up for success from the start.

In response to common problems Estelle noticed across different parts of the social purpose sector, she developed her own project management method to support development of in-house capability. She has complemented Rock Your

Roll Out with a whole digital library of resources including learning modules, masterclasses and 'Critical Friend' training.

Estelle brings three careers to the table: music education, public administration and consultancy. For 25 years she has supported others to achieve their best and make the difference they desire.

Estelle is also a self-professed learning and continuous improvement junkie. She is a Graduate of the Australian Institute of Company Directors and also holds a Bachelor of Music (Hons), a Master of Arts and an Executive Master of Public Administration, all from the University of Melbourne. Add to that a Certificate in Personal and Business Coaching and a Churchill Fellowship.

Estelle lives in Melbourne, Australia and loves talking about classical music, especially opera.

Linked In – www.linkedin.com/in/estelleoc/

www.ingramcontent.com/pod-product-compliance
Lightning Source LLC
Chambersburg PA
CBHW062025290426
44108CB00025B/2789